Foreword

"Some people enter your life for a reason" - Everyone.

I am thankful till this day the invitation I received to his table the night open-mic was packed at the Sappho Cafe in Glebe, AUS. If it wasn't for the hospitable individual that Vito is, I probably would have been standing all night in the middle of all the people sitting down feeling extremely awkward. Therefore, it is my honour to write this letter. My study abroad experience would have not been completed if I did not meet the insightful being that he is.

I was fortunate enough to get to know Vito in depth and grasp his life story during an interview I did of him for an assignment I had to do for university. Geez, his life has many unfoldings. With a life background such as his, it is easy to understand why the philosophy of life and human connection is an important value to learn. It also demonstrates the possibility of going from rags-to-riches-- although Vito would probably replace riches with comfort because life is much more becoming rich. Regardless of an individual's upbringing with persistence, determination, purpose, and hard work anything is possible and Vito's life story is a clear example. His life with chickens is one that demonstrates the grind of life and teaches one valuable lessons. One in particular, "create the world you want to live in. Create, create, create. Creativity can be anything, don't stop creating."

Thank you for this lesson and thank you for living the life you did and using it as a source to tell stories and a tool to create a better world. Last but not least, thank you for your energy and the nourishing of my mind.

Much love,
Elizabeth Villagomez
August 2019

"This book is dedicated to my father, Giuseppe Radice and my mother, Angela Martone without whom I would not exist!"

-Don Vito Radice
7th August 2019

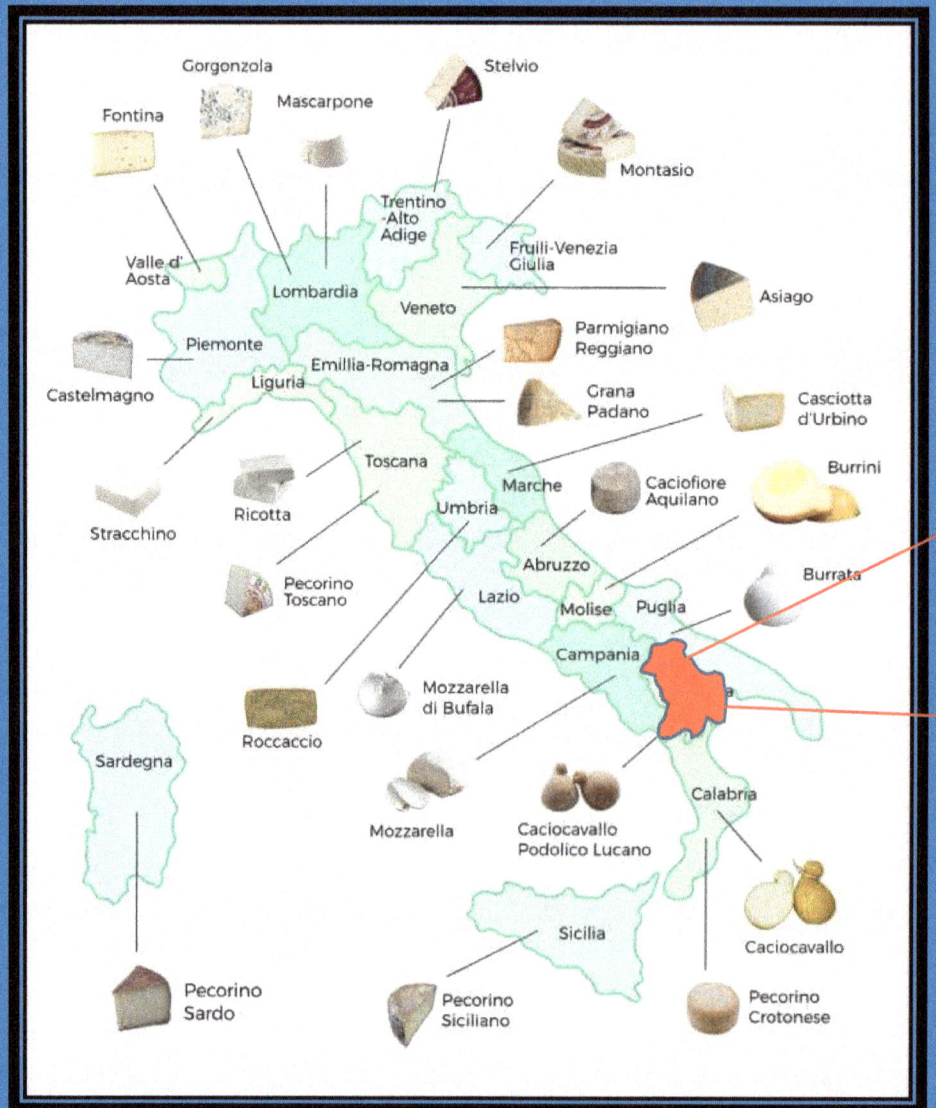

To Get in touch with the author:

"The Polemicist":
controversial, argumentative, adversarial, agitator, non-conformist, oppositional, enigmatic, agent provocateur, "international man of mystery", trouble-maker, shit-stirrer.

Email: vitoradice@gmail.com
Facebook: Vito Radice
Instagram: don_vito_radice
Website: buonavitabecreative.com
Mobile: 0490 012 461

Contents:
Part 1: The Old World
(The days of innocence/The "Halcyon Days")

Chapter 1: My Father: Giuseppe Radice
Chapter 2: My Mother: Angela (Martone) Radice
Chapter 3: My Story Begins……The Farm: DIFESA
Chapter 4: The Sea Voyage

Part 2: The New World
(The "Lucky Country"/The land of "Milk and Honey")

Chapter 5: The New Land: The Journey Begins
Chapter 6: My Story Continues……
Chapter 7: School Days
Chapter 8: My Life with Chickens!
Chapter 9: Sydney: A simpler Time!
Chapter 10: Death, God, Religion, Love and Masturbation!
Chapter 11: Family Time! A Bonding Time!
Chapter 12: The Golden Chariot
Chapter 13: In the End…

Part 1: The Old World
(The Days of Innocence/The "Halcyon Days")

"I Pity the Poor Immigrant"

I pity the poor immigrant
Who wishes he would've stayed home
Who uses all his power to do evil
But in the end is always left so alone
That man whom with his fingers cheats
And who lies with every breath
Who passionately hates his life
And likewise, fears his death.

I pity the poor immigrant
Whose strength is spent in vain
Whose heaven is like ironsides
Whose tears are like rain
Who eats but is not satisfied
Who hears but does not see
Who falls in love with wealth itself
And turns his back on me.
I pity the poor immigrant
Who tramples through the mud
Who fills his mouth with laughing
And who builds his town with blood
Whose visions in the final end
Must shatter like the glass
I pity the poor immigrant
When his gladness comes to pass!

Songwriter: Bob Dylan

Chapter 1: My Father: Giuseppe Radice

My father was a very simple man. He only wanted a simple and uncomplicated life.

He liked fresh air and sheep. He did not like people or the company of people much. *"Never trust the people"* was his mantra and he repeated this often. (maybe this is where I get my love of repeating words and phrases over and over again, to the point that Mariclaire only allows me to repeat things three times and Sheila ONLY twice!).

Giuseppe was born in a small Italian village called *San Fele* in the province of *Basilicata* on 10th September 1924. Until 1960 he lived a simple life as a subsistence farmer (with his father Nicola, the patriarch and Sozomeno, his brother), working the land, milking the cow, looking after the sheep and going off to the village (which was about six kilometres away) on his beloved donkey.

San Fele, Basilicata, Italia

He was not much of a thinker or interested in learning. He in fact only had six months of schooling, preferring to run away and sleep under the *"Ponte Vecchio"*, where he was often found, rather than sit in a classroom. These were his halcyon days. His days of *"milk and honey"*. He would often reminisce about these days when he was not angry and throwing a tantrum. He could be "light" and cheerful, even funny and sometimes he even laughed, when he wanted to. But these times were very few a far between. For the man that I knew was a bitter and angry man, not the young boy sleeping under the *"Ponte Vecchio"*!

It was in 1960 that Giuseppe's whole world came tumbling down. Destroyed forever! He was told by his father that the farm could no longer sustain three families, someone had to leave and since he was the eldest, he had to go! He cried! *"Why me?"* he screamed to my grandfather. *"Your brother has problems with his passport. It has to be you!"*. He ran away to the place that had been his sanctuary, under the *"Ponte Vecchio"*.

He was persuaded that life in "Australia" would be the best thing for him and his family, especially for his two young boys Nick and Vito. That this was NOT about his needs but to provide a BETTER future for them. Australia was the FUTURE! He cried even more! He cried because he knew he would NEVER come back! That this was FOREVER! A lifetime jail sentence for a crime he didn't know he had committed!

So, it came to pass that in 1960, Giuseppe left his beloved farm, *"Difesa"*, bordered the Achilles Laura ocean liner, the *"Marconi"* and came to Australia.

Bare in mind that Giuseppe had never seen the sea before. Let alone an enormous ship, on which he spent thirty-nine days for the journey to Australia.

1: Father, 1959
2: Father's birth details
3: Father, Nick (brother), mother, me, 1960
4: Brother, mother, me, 1961

1: Nonna Angela Radice and Nonno Nicolo Radice
2: Nonna Angela Radice and Nonno Nicolo Radice in Difesa
3: Nonno Nicola Radice in front of the old farmhouse
4: Zia Rosa Radice and Nonna Angela Radice in front of the old farmhouse
5: Nonna Angela Radice in front of the old farmhouse
6: Nonna Angela Radice in the vegetable garden

Chapter 2: My Mother: Angela (Martone) Radice

My mother was born on 5th May 1932. She married my father in 1950. She was just eighteen years old! My father was twenty-six years old.

Her family suffered through quite a few tragedies. Two of her brothers died early in their lives, Michael died when he was nine years old from appendicitis and Giuseppe died from a work place accident (he fell into a vat of molten metal) in Canada. He was twenty-six years old. Her youngest brother, Antonio had a nervous breakdown when he was eighteen years, from which he never fully recovered.

Her parents, Vito Martone (after whom I was named) and Angelamaria Martone (Carnevale) were the kindest people in the village. Everyone knew of them, respected and loved them. My grandfather, Nonno Vito, was nicknamed *(supranomo)*, *"Skertz"*, which loosely translated means "joker". Something which I seem to have inherited! He made everyone laugh and also made the best wine in the region.

My grandfather on my father's side, Nonno Nicolo, was nicknamed *(supranomo)*, *"Feffo"*, which loosely translated means "fool"!

People were referred to by the their *supranomo*, *"Nicolo U'Feffo, Vito Skertz"*.

These *supranomi* always seemed to refer to some derogatory aspects of that individual. The ones I remember were:

"Pisca Latte", Piss Milk,
"Sansa Sange", Without Blood,
"Morta Letto", Dead in Bed.

In those days, people didn't get married for love, they were arranged marriages. The parents of the boy would approach parents of the girl (usually the father) and ask if he was interested in marrying his daughter off to his son. The girl had no say in it! Land or money was usually involved in the discussions. It was a business transaction

At twenty-six years of age, my father was getting quite old and was not really interested in getting married. Nonno Nicola, had other ideas and knew that if he didn't marry Giuseppe off soon, it would become more difficult as he got older.

So, the deal was made!

Angela Martone married Giuseppe Radice and became Angela Radice.

My mother has often told me that when she married my father:

"I went from Heaven to Hell!"

My mother has since to told me that she asked her father, *"Why did you marry me off to him?"* His reply, *"I didn't know! I'm sorry!"*

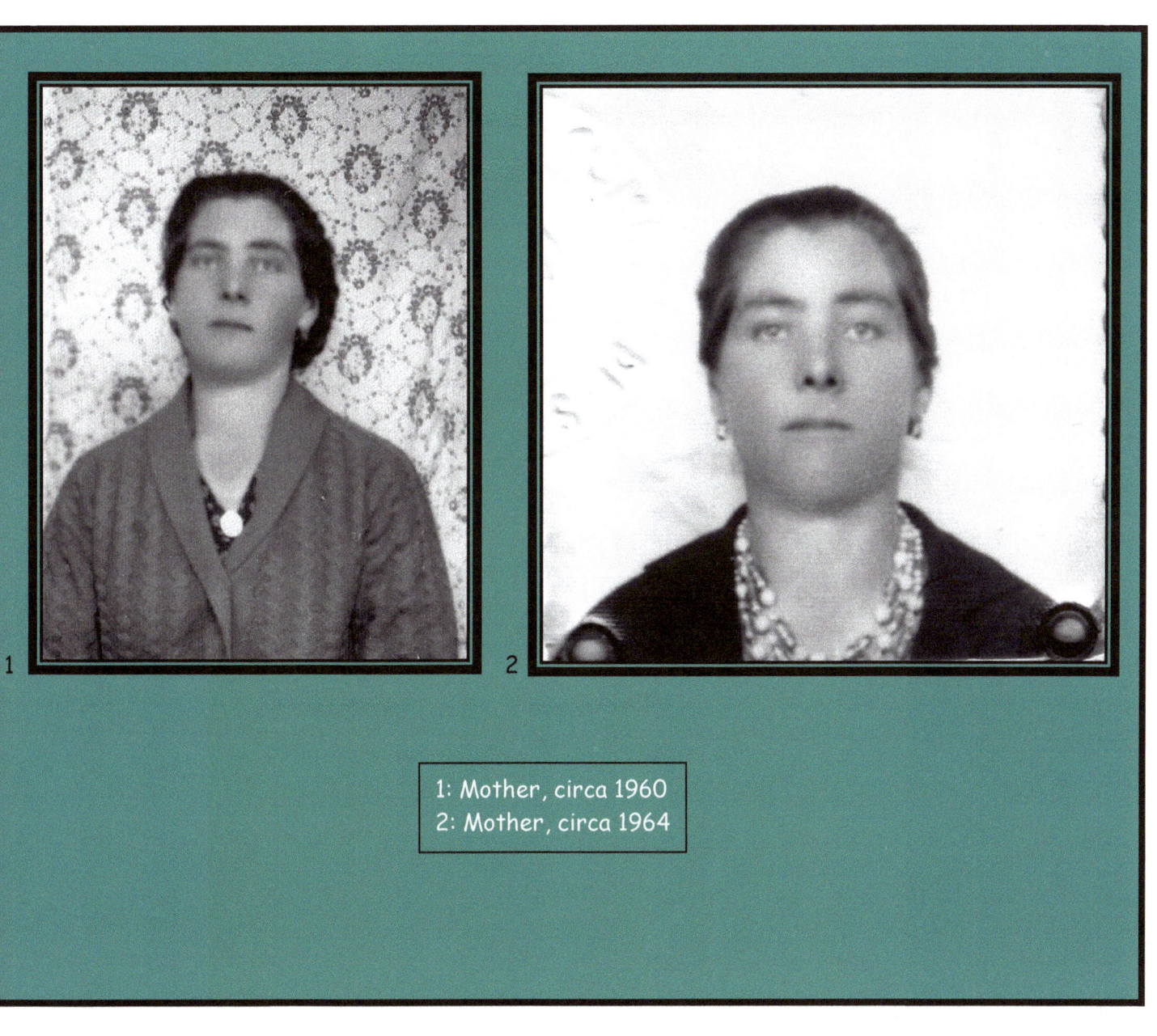

1: Mother, circa 1960
2: Mother, circa 1964

Mother and Father on their wedding day, she was 18 and he was 26 years old, 1950

1: Nonna Angelamaria Martone and Nonno Vito Martone
2: Zio Antonio Martone, Nonna Angelamaria Martone and Nonno Vito Martone
3: Zio Giuseppe Martone died in an accident in Canada in 1959
4: Mother and brother Nick at about 2 years old

Chapter 3: My Story Begins……The Farm: DIFESA

I was born on the 10th March 1959, in the Year of the Pig of the Chinese calendar, under the Astrological Sign of Pisces. I was born in the village of *San Fele*, in my Nonna Martone's house. The house is built into the side of the mountain and it's still there today. Abandoned!

My father wanted a boy and told her, "If it's not a boy, do not come back!". My mother tells me that she always wanted a girl and had hoped I would be a girl but God was not kind to her and instead she got me, another boy! This did not stop her though and apparently she would dress me in girls' clothes as a baby. Apparently I was very cute and adorable. Whom am I to argue?

Me at 18 months, 1960

The area of Basilicata that our farm was located in was called *"Difesa"*. According to a story my uncle Sozomeno told me, the reason why it was called this was that during the second world War, this area was the last line of defence or resistance against the Germans, *"Defence (English) Difesa"*.

There were two mountains directly to the right of the homestead, *"Pierno"* and *"Santa Croce"*.

We lived in a very simple three room building on a hill, my grandfather in the middle room, my uncle on the left side room and we had the right. We all lived in this one room. We cooked, ate and slept in this one room. Each contained a fireplace on which we cooked and the fire kept us warm. There was no internal water, which had to be fetched from a nearby well and no electricity. We used oil lamps to provide lighting at night which provided very little light and made the room quite dark and sooty.

Original "Off Grid Living"!

Electricity was being rolled into our region when we left in 1964, as we were leaving!

The old farmhouse in Difesa, 1960. It was demolished in 1983.

There were no toilets, showers or laundries of any sort. We had to do our ablutions behind the building. Washing ourselves and our clothes was done in the river, about a twenty-minute walk away.

One particular event that I remember vividly was when we had to have the baby calf in the room with us for almost a month. There were cow thieves targeting our region and under the cloak of darkness, they would go around to the different farms and whilst everyone was asleep, steal calves and lambs. So to protect our valued calf, she lived with us. I actually liked it. She was very friendly and had kind eyes. Although, the smell of her poo was sometimes overbearing for my tender nostrils.

My grandfather was a hard task master and would make the family work on the farm from dawn till dusk seven days a week, summer and winter, every year. The summers were extremely hot and the winters were extremely cold. There were no machines to make the physical work any easier. Everything was done by hand, using very simple, ancient techniques, passed down through the generations. That's the way things were done, there was no point arguing or questioning it.

In spring and summer work was in ploughing, sowing, harvesting, staking and slaughtering. In the winter months it involved clearing the land which was not very fertile and full of rocks which had to be removed.

Everyone was involved in this work.

The land was worked with a wooden plough pulled along by a cow, just as in the Roman days. The wheat was sown by hand. The wheat was harvested by hand using a sickle and then bagged by hand. The hay was rolled by hand, moved by hand and stacked in the barn by hand.

Most of the wheat was sold off and the rest (the lower quality stuff, husks etc.) was left for our consumption. The wheat was ground by hand using two large stones to grind it down.

Cows and goats milk was used to make cheese, which was predominantly sold with very little left for us. Pigs, lambs, chickens, rabbits, turkeys, pigeons, were slaughtered and the meat sold off. The off cuts and the offal was left for us to make salami, *"copa,"*, *"prosciutto"*, ham, pigs trotters and other cured meats.

No part of the slaughtered animal was thrown away. The blood was collected and eaten, the fat was used as lard for cooking, the offal was cooked and eaten.

Two delicacies of our region are *"Sfritt"*, a dish cooked after the slaughter of a pig. This was a big affair and involved at least eight men to hold it down. The pig was an enormous animal. It knew it was going to die a very horrible death. It did not want to die! After exsanguination, the draining of all of the pig's blood, it was collected and later cooked and eaten!

The festivities lasted all day and well into the night and most of the villagers came to celebrate and have a good time. *"Au'Sfrit"* was cooked around lunchtime and everyone claimed to have the BEST recipe. The basic ingredients common to all were: pig offal, pig blood, potatoes, onions, garlic and red capsicum in vinegar, all fried in a huge by pan, usually by a man, the owner of the pig. Of course there were many variations of this.

The second delicacy was a *"blood cake"*. This was served in the evening with coffee as a dessert. The main ingredients were, fresh pig's blood, chocolate, sugar, milk cinnamon and other spices, all put into a cake pastry, with cross-work pastry strips on top and baked in the oven for about twenty minutes.

Both dishes were delicious!

Bread was made only once a month because it required a lot of wood to heat the stone oven. So once it was fired, enough bread was baked to last the whole month. Pizzas, frittatas *(an Italian omelette)*, sweets other foods were also cooked. Other nearby friends were also invited to use the fired up oven to bake their bread as well. So *"baking day"* was also a day of festivity and celebration

A story my mother loves to tell me was on one particularly hot summer day, when she was working the fields, she decided to send me back to the homestead with *"Sargente"* our dog. He was black and quite large and I must've been about 3 years old. My mother used to take me with her when she worked the fields because there was no one to look after me since everyone else was also out working the fields. She could see me walking with *Sargente* who would push me back in the right direction if I started to wander. She found me sleeping on *Sargente's* belly, who was also sleeping, underneath the cherry tree in front of the homestead.

Another time my mother gave me a piece of bread to eat, a little while later, she came back came and was surprised that I had already finished it so quickly. Apparently. *Sargente* had gently teased it out of my had with his teeth, ate it and then lay beside me sheepishly pretending to be innocent!

I loved *Sargente*. He was still alive when we left in 1964. I believe he lived a long life.

1

2

3

4

5

Life on the farm
Previous page:
4: Zia Rossa, 5: Zio Sozomeno,
6: Zio Francesco
This page:
1 & 2: Mammanonna Radice,
4 & 5: Zio Sozomeno

Photos circa 1970

Chapter 4: The Sea Voyage

We spent a night in Naples with my grandparents *"Papanonno e Mamanonna d'paese, grandfather and grandmother from the village"*, (where we had to board the Ship. I had never left my village, let along seen a massive city like Naples or a huge ocean liner.
I remember being very sad and crying because I didn't want to leave my grandparents (I was very close to them and I loved them a lot)!

On board we were placed in a four persons cabin with a solitary porthole window which we shared with another woman I'd never met before. It was very small and cramped but I had the top bunk so I was happier!

My brother and I were in complete awe at the size and grandeur of the ship. We had never seen anything like this. We used to get up really in the mornings and rush out for breakfast before anybody else was there. Laid out on an extremely long table, there were trays and trays heaped with food that we had never seen before! We used to just stand and stare at it trying to see if we could recognise anything. We did not!

The ocean was very rough at times and a lot of people got seasick. Fortunately, my brother and I did not and we would go off and explore the ship, when he felt kindly towards me. At other times he would go off on his own and I would be left with my mother. My brother is seven years older than me!

There were many stories from our journey but one particular one which sticks in my memory was the stormy night when a rumour spread through the ship that an inspection of all the cabins was going to take place. Apparently, people had smuggled on board cakes of cheese and jars of salami, assuming that these would not be available in Australia. So in the middle of this dark, windy and stormy night with the ship rocking from side to side and water splashing onto the decks, rows of drenched women, dressed in black, clinging for their lives, tossed it all overboard.

There was no inspection!

We went through the Suez Canal and the trip lasted thirty-three days.

"The Weeping Song"

Go son, go down to the water
And see the women weeping there
Then go up into the mountains
The men, they are weeping too
Father, why are all the women weeping
They are weeping for their men
Then why are all the men there weeping
They are weeping back at them
This is a weeping song
A song in which to weep
While all the men and women sleep
This is a weeping song
But I won't be weeping long
Father, why are all the children weeping
They are merely crying son
Oh are they merely crying, father
Yes, true weeping is yet to come
This is a weeping song
A song in which to weep
While all the men and children sleep
This is a weeping song
But I won't be weeping long
Oh father tell me, are you weeping'
Your face seems wet to touch
Oh then I'm so sorry, father
I never thought I hurt you so much
This is a weeping song
A song in which to weep
While we rock ourselves to sleep
This is a weeping song
But I won't be weeping long
But I won't be weeping long
But I won't be weeping long
But I won't be weeping long

Performed by: <u>Nick Cave and The Bad Seeds</u>
Songwriter: Nick Cave

Part 2: The New World
(The "Lucky Country"/The Land of "Milk and Honey")

"Immigrant Song"

Ah-ah, ah!
Ah-ah, ah!
We come from the land of the ice and snow
From the midnight sun, where the hot springs flow
The hammer of the gods
We'll drive our ships to new lands
To fight the horde, and sing and cry
Valhalla, I am coming!
On we sweep with threshing oar
Our only goal will be the western shore.
Ah-ah, ah!
Ah-ah, ah!
We come from the land of the ice and snow
From the midnight sun where the hot springs flow
How soft your fields so green
Can whisper tales of gore
Of how we calmed the tides of war
We are your overlords.
On we sweep with threshing oar
Our only goal will be the western shore.
So now you'd better stop and rebuild all your ruins
For peace and trust can win the day despite of all your losing.
Ooh-ooh, ooh-ooh, ooh-ooh
Ooh-ooh, ooh-ooh, ooh-ooh
Ooh-ooh, ooh-ooh, ooh-ooh
Ooh-ooh, ooh-ooh, ooh-ooh
Ooh-ooh, ooh-ooh, ooh-ooh

Songwriters: Jimmy Page / Robert Plant
Performed by: Led Zeppelin

Chapter 5: The New Land: The Journey Begins

On his arrival to *"The New Land"*, he lived with my uncle (his brother-in-law), Zio Michaele Carnevale and his sister, my aunty, Zia Laura

My uncle was one of the very first to immigrate out to Australia, coming here in 1952, where he settled in Five Dock (an inner west suburb of Sydney). He had a vision and passion to get his *"paesane, (person or persons from the same village that are not directly related)*, out of the squalor and poverty of *San Fele*.

At the time, the Australian Government required a *"Sponser"* for someone to immigrate. The *"Sponser"* needed to provide two requirements for approval: shelter and a job for six months. This what he provided to numerous *"San Felese"*. My father being one of these. My uncle was a conduit for many people to make a new life in *"The Lucky Country"*.

The house was located in Janet Street, Five Dock Sydney Australia (which later was subsumed by The Department of Education, knocked down and become the oval for "Drummoyne Boys' High School", (which later was sold off to build townhouses on). The job was at *"Lysaght Wire and Steel Foundry"* located in Abbotsford, Sydney NSW.

My father often told me that:

"I went from Heaven to Hell!"

This is what my father would often tell me of his experience when first arriving in Australia.

The *"Hell"* he was referring to was working in a factory for ten hours a day, five days a week, without ever seeing the sun! There was plenty of *"overtime"* for anyone who had the *"balls"* to work even more! My father had very big *"balls"*! If this was not *"Hell"* enough, his work was in the foundry section, where molten metal (of temperatures exceeding five hundred degrees Celsius), were poured into moulds.

This was truly **"HELL"** for my father!

As part of his immigration entry requirements, he had to attend English classes two nights a week, Tuesday and Thursday from 6pm to 9pm, every week. My father was almost completely illiterate in his first language (having only six

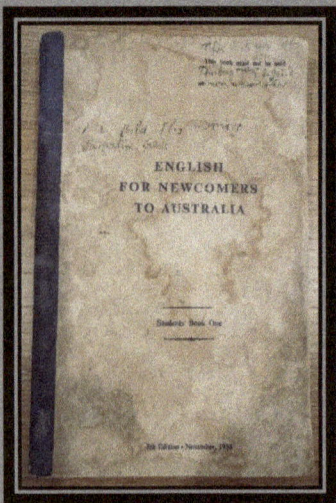
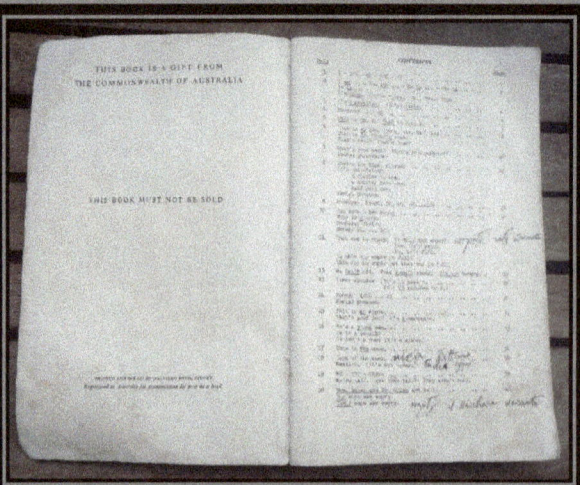

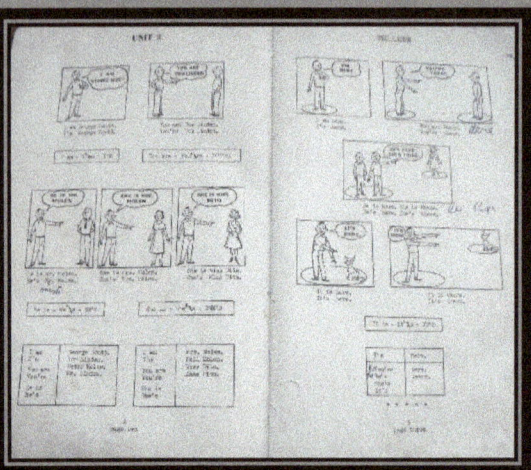
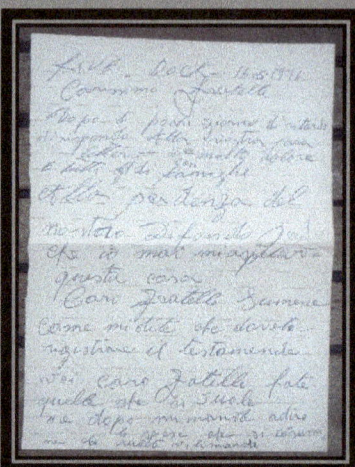
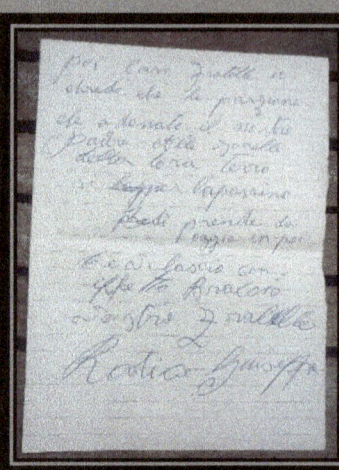
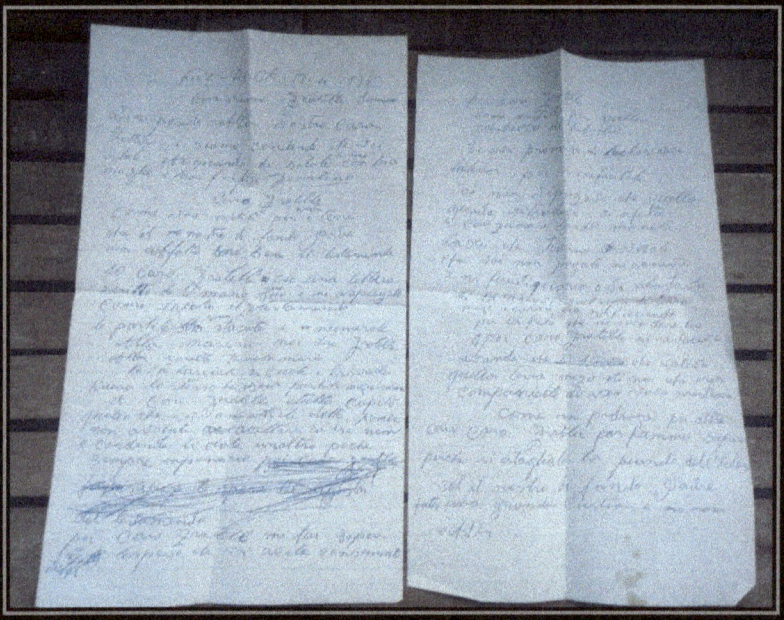
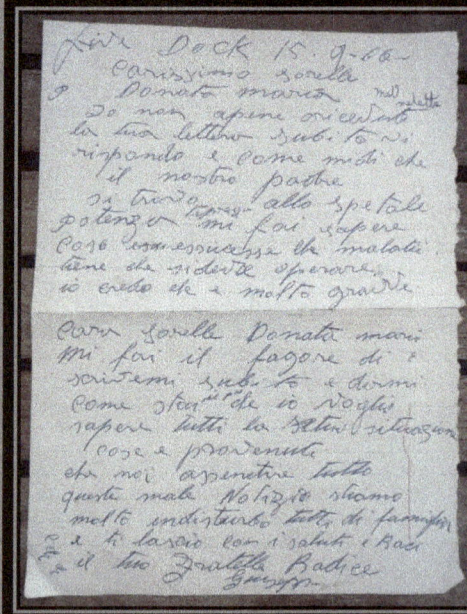

1, 2, 3 and 4: New immigrants English book
5, 6 and 7: Letters from my father to his brother Zio Sozomeno Radice
8: Letter from my father to his sister Zia Donatamaria Russo

1   2

All photos 1960-1964 at Zio Michaele's house, 46 Janet Street Five Dock, Sydney Australia

3   4

1: Father in backyard
2: Father in front yard

5: Zia Laura and Zio Michaele
6: Great Uncle Giuseppe and Cousin Joe

5   6

3: Cousin Joe Carnevale, Zia Laura, Father and Great Uncle Guiseppe Carnevale
4: Great Uncle, Uncle Michaele and Zia Laura in front of the new Chrysler Valiant

months of education in Italian). So, this was a Herculean feat for him, but he persevered and his English was actually not too bad……when he wanted use it!

Being alone meant that he a freedom to do whatever he wanted. The only other time he had this level of freedom was when was conscripted into the Italian Army in 1939 to fight the Allies. Italy was on the *"Other Side"* with the Germans early on in WWII, where he was sent to Bologna to "peel" potatoes. Then ran away and fled when the Germans came! He was actually classified as a traitor until Italy jumped the fence and joined the Americans to fight against the Germans *(but that's another story)*.

With his best friend, Compare Jerry Di Giacomo (*Compare* is *Godfather*, Jerry is my *Godfather*), they terrorised the streets of Five Dock and Drummoyne much to the chagrin and annoyance of my uncle. Nevertheless, he was able to accumulate enough money for a deposit on a house in Five Dock, ready for us to move straight into when we arrived from Italy.

If nothing else, my father was a very proud man!

Everything had changed for him. Even his name was changed. He was no longer called Giuseppe, he was now Joe!

When we arrived from Italy my father was on Christmas holidays from *Lysaght* and had found a temporary job at *Toohey's Brewery* located in Mary Street Surry Hills, where *The World Square* is now. (It moved in 1975 to its current location in Nyrang Street Lidcombe).

He liked it so much that he quickly resigned from *Lysaght* and went to work at *Toohey's* all of his working life until he retired in 1989.

My father was an angry and bitter man. He was very dominating and very violent (physically and psychologically) and abusive both to my mother and to me.

When I was about six years old he hit me with a belt. I still have the scars on my back. I don't remember the situation but I do remember tears running down my face and being angry as hell. I swore to him that I would get him back at him one day. I would enact my revenge.

I did *(but that's another story)*!

1

2

3

4

5

6

1: Mother with her sister, Zia Donatamaria Tronnolone from Adelaide
2: Zia Donatamaria, father and mother in the backyard of the house in Five Dock
3: Zio Antonio Tronnolone, Nick, Zia, mother, cousin Mary, father (back row) (front row) cousin Vito, me and cousin Pat
4: Zio Antonio, Zia Donatamaria, mother and father next to the old garage
5: Nick, Mary, Vito, me and Pat
6: Zio Michaele, Zia Laura, mother, me, father and Nick

All photos circa 1967- 1968

All photos circa 1967-1968

1: Nick and me at the front of the Five Dock house
2: Nick and me in the backyard
3: Nick, father, mother and me at Zio Michaele's new house, Potts St., Gladesville
4: Me, father, mum's cousin Vincenza Di Giacomo, mum and Vincenza's son, Anthony
5: Nick in front of the TV and the record player (on his left)
6: Me in front of the TV and the "K-Tell Record-O-Matic"

He was a doctor, prosecutor, judge and jury all in one. He could and would determine the fate of a person instantly. There was no need for elaborate court cases or the presumption of being innocent before being proven guilty. He could tell is someone was guilty with absolutely no information or evidence. Let's face it, everyone is guilty of something. He didn't need evidence. That was all irrelevant. He just knew. It was like a sixth sense.

They were guilty!

Case closed.

Hang them!

If you had facial hair, long hair, matted hair, coloured hair, sculptured hair, no hair, unkept hair, dishevelled clothes, dirty clothes, torn clothes, skimpy clothes, no clothes, tattoos, body piercings, too much jewellery, hippies, bodgies, bikies, atheists, non-Catholics and anyone coloured, were all guilty!

Most people from southern Italy were very superstitious and practised weird rituals and my father was no different. These included doing things by the phases of the moon such as: cutting his hair, toe nails, making wine, killing animals, pruning trees which were all done when the moon was waning. Planting seeds or anything connected to growth was don when the moon was waxing.

He also had the crazy idea that he could tell if someone was gossiping about him. He would Say *"tange nu frisce in da vrecchio"*, I have a whistle in my ear. If it was in the left ear it was bad, if it was in the right ear it was good. Then he would say *"counte, counte"*, count until he would say stop, when the whistling stopped, then using that number, say 6, he would count to the 6th letter of the alphabet "F". He would search for a person's name or *supronomo* that started with "F", after a few seconds he would shout out *"Fresce"*, he was convinced that this person was talking about him!

He also had some great sayings which just don't do them justice when they are translated into English:

- *"Sere sere, vadgnio, vadgnio. A tripe mia stia sampre diggiona!"*,
  (Hill, hill, valley, valley. My stomach is always empty!)
  This was said after a hearty meal, especially if someone asked you if the meal was satisfying and you were full.
  (Apparently, it's about a goat!)

- *"Qunada a borsa a borsa! Quanda a bovila a bovila!"*
  (When you go for bags, you go for bags! When you go for butterflies, you go for butterflies!)
  This was said when you are doing something or going somewhere and some point there is a new choice or direction presented to you.

- *"Voglio andare a postare una lettera!"*
  (I want to go and post a letter!)
  This was said straight after lunch when you wanted to be excused to go to the toilet.

- *"Primo de domanini!"*
  (Before tomorrow!)
  This was said when you very EXCITED about doing something and couldn't wait.)

- *"Posse suspirare!"*
  (I can breathe!)
  This was said when he came back to his house @ 16 Elizabeth Street, Five Dock.

- *"Non Posse suspirare!"*
  (I cannot breathe!)
  This was said when he was at someone else's house!

- *"Casa mia bella!"*
  (My beautiful house!)
  This was said when he came back to his house in Elizabeth Street, Five Dock.

He loved his house in Elizabeth Street, Five Dock!

1, 2: The backyard garden in the Five Dock house.

Photos taken by Mariclaire Pringle, 14.07.2019

Chapter 6: My Story Continues……

I was almost six years old when I arrived in Sydney on the 24th December 1964. I came with my mother and brother from a small village (called *"San Fele"*) in Italy where I was born.

We came over on an ocean liner called the *"Galileo"* and that's when I met my father for the very first time. He had been here since 1960. I remember this day vividly, as if it were just yesterday. The ship docked at Circular Quay and I was trying to see my father, but of course I had no idea what he looked like, but somehow I still thought I would be able to recognise him from the many faces standing and cheering on the wharf.

Finally, we disembarked and somehow amongst the throng I was introduced to my father. I shook his hand, (our family never openly demonstrated love and affection with each other)!

My uncle was also there. He drove us to our new home (Elizabeth Street, Five Dock) in his brand new 1964 Chrysler Valiant Triptronic with wings.

It was Christmas Eve!

The Galileo Ocean Liner
SS Galileo Galilei was an ocean liner built in 1963.
She was scuttled in the Strait of Malacca in 1999.

Chapter 7: School Days

"School Days"

Up in the mornin' and out to school
The teacher is teachin' the Golden Rule
American history and practical math
You studyin' hard and hopin' to pass
Workin' your fingers right down to the bone
And the guy behind you won't leave you alone
Ring, ring goes the bell
The cook in the lunch room's ready to sell
You're lucky if you can find a seat
You're fortunate if you have time to eat
Back in the classroom, open your books
Keep up the teacher don't know how mean she looks
Soon as three o'clock rolls around
You finally lay your burden down
Close up your books, get out of your seat
Down the halls and into the street
Up to the corner and 'round the bend
Right to the juke joint, you go in
Drop the coin right into the slot
You're gotta hear somethin' that's really hot
With the one you love, you're makin' romance
All day long you been wantin' to dance,
Feeling the music from head to toe
Round and round and round we go
Hail, hail rock and roll
Deliver me from the days of old
Long live rock and roll
The beat of the drums, loud and bold
Rock, rock, rock and roll
The feelin' is there, body and soul.

Songwriter: Chuck Berry

My first day at Five Dock Primary school was a very traumatic experience for my brother and I. My mother's cousin who was supposed to take us didn't come so we went off by ourselves, both having absolutely no English knowledge at all.

The school was not far from our house, about a five-minute walk away.
Nick was placed into Year six of Primary School, a separate building, but still in the same grounds. I was placed in kindergarten.

There was only one simple rule in the school playground in those days and probably is still today; *"bully or be bullied!"* I was bullied! I was: *"pantsed"*, when the boy behind you in the assembly line pulled down you shorts exposing you oversized y-fronted underpants,

- called names *"Vito Mosquito"*,
- called a *"Wog"*, a derogatory term for Southern Europeans,
- ridiculed and laughed at because of the food that my mother had made for my lunch. My lunch usually consisted of two thick slices of crusty Vienna bread, filled with either, salami, Mortadella, cheese, spinach, eggplants, zucchini, onions, garlic, anchovy, capsicums, mozzarella, frittata *(Italian omelette)*.

Gourmet sandwiches today but not in 1965.

These were NOT the fillings the other kids had, which consisted predominantly of two slices of "Tip Top" white bread, containing either peanut butter or vegemite or both, all in a neat container!
Now as you can imagine, by lunchtime, my sandwiches, wrapped in butchers' paper and in my school bag for over 3 hours, had started to ferment. The smell when exposed to air was quite ripe. The other kids curious to see what I had for lunch had a field day! They fell about laughing and shouting; *"Oooooow, what is that? Are those worms? Is that shit that you're eating?"*
"Wog, Wog, Wog, Wog, Wog!"

So there was only one thing to do…… …..throw my lunch in the bin!

I went without lunch!

Oh, how I wished to have lunch like everyone else!

One lunchtime, my teacher who was on playground duty, noticed that I wasn't eating, she might have even seen me throw my food into the bin. I'm not sure. She came over to where I was sitting and asked me where my lunch was, of course, I couldn't answer. I could see in her eyes and face that she didn't require an answer, so she walked off and a few minutes later came back and handed me a meat pie.

My very first meat pie ever!

I loved it!

Nick took no shit from anyone and he quickly asserted his position in the primary school. The head bully picked on him one day but Nick was not one to back down from a fight and quickly jumped on him, put his ear into his mouth and bit it. The boy was screaming and crying and there was blood everywhere!

My parents were called to the school. The boy and his ear were all fine.

Nick was NEVER bullied again!

The story quickly spread throughout the entire school.

I was safe………until he left for high school! Then I was fucked again!

Since I was not a fighter like Nick, the only option I felt I had for me not to be bullied was……. to be THE BEST! To be the best and excel at everything, both academic and sport!

To be the smartest, the fastest, the most creative!

Whatever it was I become SUPER competitive!

I took no prisoners!

No one stood in my way!

And I SUCEEDED!

I was no longer bullied! I was looked up to and admired!

Respected even!

My best friend was Phillip Berry, a true blue Aussie. He lived on James Street, the second house up from the water at *"Hen and Chicken Bay"*, Five Dock. He had four older brothers (all with long, straight black hair) and an older sister. His father worked (I never knew what he did) but his mother did not and stayed at home.

I loved his family! I often would wish that I was his brother and had been born into his family! They were the complete opposite to my family and everything we did. They seemed normal to me and we were not!

They loved Rugby league and he was a very good player. He was selected for the Western Suburbs region and for the state. I was just as good but was not allowed to play. My father was never one for sport, seeing it as waste of time and money, especially Rugby League, which he thought was way too rough and that I would get hurt.

Phillip supported *"Canterbury Bankstown"*, (in fact his whole family did), which at the time were called *"The Berries"*, which explains why he went for them *(today they are called "The Bulldogs", "The Berries" was obviously too soft for the modern era)*. They were also my team for a short time until I started supporting The *"St George Dragons"* or simply *"The Dragons"* or *"Saints"*. Probably because their colours were red and white (red was my favourite colour) or because all they had on the jersey was a big, red "V" (V for Vito)!

I was a "Latch-Key Kid", both my parents went off to work very early in the mornings and arrived late in the afternoons, so my mother tied the house key around the shoulder strap of my singlet and was left to fend on my own in the mornings and afternoons.

My mother's first job was as a "piece-meal" worker at *"Kolotex"*, a hosiery mill in George street, Leichhardt, owen by the Kornmehl Family. Basically it was a "sweat-shop" where women worked on machines or sowed by hand. My mother sowed by hand. The more items you sowed the more bonuses your team got. All the sowers were women! All the "leading-hands" & bosses were men! They pushed the women very hard and were very authoritarian and competitive. The women were not allowed to talk to each other or take breaks.

She started work at 7:30am in the morning and finished at 4:30pm in the afternoon with a ten-minute break for morning and afternoon tea and half an hour for lunch. They had to "bundy on and off" each morning and afternoon. They would be docked pay if they arrived late or left early. A hooter went off at the start and finish of the day. It was very rigid! *("Bundying on and off" was very common in labouring factories, where workers had a time-sheet which had to be stamped on, at the start of the day and stamped off, at the end of the day. If you did not get it stamped, you did not get pay. If you were late ten minutes or left 10 minutes early, your pay was cut, "docked" by half an hour!)*

My mother HATED it!

This is the Kolotex factory in George Street, Leichhardt, taken in the late 1960s at 10.55am. The Time Clock ("Bundy Clock") is on the left hand corner wall.

Mornings were particularly stressful for me as I didn't know when to go to school. I was in a dilemma: If I went TOO early I would be the only one there, if I went TOO late, I would have missed valuable time playing with my friends. I neither had a watch or could tell the time. So, I devised a simple strategy: our backyard and driveway was made of concrete, I would run and jump, if I landed in a square: time to go, if I landed on the dividing line between tow squares: it was not time to go.

The method seemed to work very well!

The driveway separated our house with our next door neighbour's house and there was no fence separating the two houses until the backyard started. *"The Wade"* family lived there until the early 1970s. They had two children (a boy and girl) who were both sent to boarding school. Mrs Wade stayed at home and Mr Wade went to work (I never really knew what he did, although I think he was a lawyer).

Their kitchen window was very low and overlooked our driveway and since there was no fence dividing the two properties I was able to reach up and talk to Mrs Wade when she was doing the cooking for dinner. Many an afternoon was spent standing at her window talking to her. I loved Mrs wade. She was kind, warm, intelligent supportive and full of love for everyone. She would encourage me to study and be creative and I learnt a lot from her. In fact, my interest in art, especially drawing and painting, was started by her.

One day she gave me a set of watercolour paints which I loved so much and quickly started painting all sorts of things. I remember painting the side of her house with the kitchen window and Mrs Wade at it, looking out. She loved that painting so much so that I gave it to her and she hung it up on her kitchen wall, directly opposite the window, so I could see it when I looked in.

I was SO proud!

I wanted to be part of her family too!

Our house had an outside toilet *"outside dunny", ("dunny" is Australian slang for toilet)*, it still does today. It has no electricity, so it was a very traumatic experience for me when I had to go to the toilet in the middle of a dark night. Opposite the toilet was a very old, huge wooden barn/workshop/garage, with massive wooden old doors. I would try to keep it in as much as possible but eventually I would succumb and rush outside. I would try to be as fast as I could but nevertheless it was always a very scary. I always thought that I could see shapes in the shadows and darkness through the barn door which sometimes was left open. Sometimes I would close my eyes and pretend that I could transport myself back into the warmth and safety of my bed. Unfortunately, I could not and had to run back as fast as I could, back to my bed. I was very terrified.

On Christmas day 1965, Mr Wade completely filled the toilet up with toys! Everyone was amazed! My father was ANGRY! He quickly blamed me for being too friendly with the Wade family. Mr Wade came over noticing that my father was unhappy and said, "Joe, Joe, these gifts are not for you, they are for your son. Don't be angry! We want to give him presents because it is Christmas time and because we want to!"

My father begrudgingly accepted their kindness but he always had this feeling he would owe them! He always had this feeling of obligation if someone gave him a gift or was invited to something. He did not understand the act and pleasure in giving or in receiving.

My father never liked getting gifts!

The best and largest present was a red scooter.

I loved that scooter.

I now had wheels!

I was mobile!

A 1950s Cyclops No. 3 scooter with shock-free foot board, parking stand and pin striping.

Chapter 8: My Life with Chickens!

"The Chicken Dance"

I don't wanna be a chicken.
I don't wanna be a duck.
So I shake my butt.

na na na na na na na na na na na na

I don't wanna be a chicken
i don't wanna be a duck so I shake my butt.
I don't wanna be a chicken.
I don't wanna be a duck.

na na na na na na na na na na na na

I don't wanna be a chicken.
I don't wanna be a duck.
So I shake my butt.
I don't wanna be a chicken.
I don't wanna be a duck.

na na na na na na na na na na na na

Songwriter: Werner Thomas

The first thing my parents did in the Five Dock house was build a chook pen at the back of the yard. My father was not a skilled builder, in fact, he was awful with the use of his hands. So, the chook pen was a mix of chicken wire as an enclosure, a wooden X-framed door covered with chicken wire, corrugated iron sheets as a roof and walls (with some hay on the floor) where the chickens could shelter and lay their eggs and the rest had a dirt floor. Nothing too flash.

It was my job to feed and collect the eggs in the morning, and to clean out the chicken pen in the evening. This involved picking up the chicken poo! I hated this job!

Once a month I would be forced to go to *"The Fresh Food Markets"* in the city on a Saturday morning at 4:30am with my dad to buy live chickens. (He liked fresh food!).

1 and 2: The Sydney fresh food markets, Haymarket,

The markets were located where the old *"Entertainment Centre"* was. The markets were demolished to make way for it and now, it has also been demolished! Who knows what is being built to replace it (apparently more apartments). Whatever it is, that place has a lot of memories and history but who will remember and tell its story?

The markets were a hive of activity, although I hated getting up at such an ungodly hour.

There was a cacophony of sounds as you entered the huge archway entrance of the building which was basically a huge covered space with all the different stalls set up in rows.

"Pannini! Si magna!", an Italian man with a tray of bread rolls stuffed with all manner of delights would walk around shouting, for anyone to buy. It was early morning and everyone was hungry (especially me). He made a rip roaring trade. Although, my father never bought me one of those eye wateringly, delicious *"pannini"*!

My father knew exactly where to go and he didn't waste any time. The live animals, such as turkeys, ducks, rabbits, were located in wire cages at the back wall of the markets nearest to the Dixon Street end.

He would buy five or six chickens, depending on the size and price. My father always haggled over the price. He had a price in his head and that was it. Nothing could dislodge him. He would haggle over ten cents. He was the best haggler I have ever seen. He loved to haggle!

We would then place the live chickens into a banana cardboard box, which had holes around it, was waxed for added strength and had a lid which we had brought with us. He had tied a rope around both ends which acted as a strap for us to hold. My father on one end, I on the other, we walked up to central bus stop, carrying our load of chickens to take the Number 437 or 438 bus back to Five Dock!

Buses in those days had conductors to collect your fare, so we had to be very careful because it was not allowed to take live animals onto a bus, especially chickens.

We would sit on the long, rear bench seat if it was a single decker bus (there were also double-decker buses) and put the box containing the live chickens underneath it.

This was an extremely traumatic and stressful bus ride!

On one particular Saturday morning, not only were the chickens making noises and pooing in the box, with its accompanying smells bad enough but they somehow managed to jump out of the box and fly throughout the bus. Luckily for us it was still very early in the morning and the bus was empty. The chickens were making a last desperate bid for freedom, aware of the fate that awaited them, which was not going to be good!

They pooed throughout the bus, on the seats, on the floor, on the windows, wherever they could they pooed! It was complete bedlam. My father and I running manically up and down the aisle trying to catch them and put them back into their box. We were able to finally recapture the escapees but not without a fierce battle. Those chickens did not want to be captured!

The conductor was very sympathetic and let us off with a warning, telling us not to bring live animals in a box onto a bus. That it was not allowed and against the law!

It was in these moments that I wished I had the superpower of *"invisibility"*!

It would have come in very handy for me!

When we arrived home, which usually was around 6:00am, it was time to kill the chickens!

> DISCLAIMER: Reader be aware: the next section contains detailed, graphic information about animal cruelty and could cause PERMANENT psychological damage! It did to me!

Once we arrived home, there was not time for breakfast! First we had to kill, pluck and wash the chickens. This was a family bonding activity! My father, my mother and myself. My brother would be excused from this activity!

The killing of the chickens was a particularly harrowing experience for me for a variety of reasons, least of which was smelling my father's farts! This just added to the whole macabre, sensory situation.

The chicken was placed in between my father's thighs, with its head hanging out. My job was to hold the chicken's legs, at an elevated forty-five degree angle, behind his back, up his backside, so that its head was lower than its feet. This was a very uncomfortable position for me because my face was almost at the same level as my father's bum (hence the farting).

With his left hand, my father would grab the chickens head and beak, with his right hand he would pluck some of the feathers from the back of its head and then with a very sharp knife cut along the ridge of the head and neck, slowly allowing the warm blood to drain of its body and into a bowl into which it was being collected.

The forty-five degree angle of elevation was extremely important in the process because it allowed gravity to drain the blood from its body while its heart was still beating and pumping the blood around its body only to be released into the bowl.

The chicken would put up a struggle, of course, but it was no match for my father's massive thighs which clenched tight around its body like a vice!

Quite often the chicken would poo at this time!

It would take about five minutes before the chicken's body became limp and we knew it was dead!

This was repeated for the remainder of the chickens and placed on a pile.

On one particular occasion, from the lifeless bodies piled on top of one another, to our utter astonishment and disbelief, a body sprang to life in front of our eyes. It sprang up as if life tried one last time to reassert itself and defeat Death. It ran around the backyard in circles, as if in a frenzied dance, with its head flopping from side to side and just as suddenly as it arose, it collapsed.

Death had won!

I guess this is where the saying; *"running around like a headless chook"* comes from!

The next step was to pluck the chickens which involved removing all the feathers. Whilst the chickens were being slaughtered a large pot of water was being boiled over an open wood fire. This was all down outside at the back of the yard in the BBQ area. The chickens were dunked into the boiling water for a few moments, pulled out and the feathers quickly plucked. There was a particular smell of the warm, wet feathers which I can still smell now.

Once all the chickens were plucked it was now time to open them up, remove the internal organs clean and wash them. Nothing was thrown away. The heart, liver, the giblet was opened up peeled of its inner lining, the intestines were split open and thoroughly washed, the bile sack was carefully cut away from the liver, this was a very delicate process because if the sack containing the bile, (which was a green colour and poisonous), was broken and contaminated the liver, it was no longer edible.

The chickens were then hung up to dry, cut up into pieces and put into the freezer.

The warm, collected blood quickly congealed from a deep burgundy turning into a deep purple black colour. This was set aside which would be later boiled for a couple of minutes in salty water. This now turned into a gun metal grey colour with holes throughout it like a sponge. This was set aside to cool, and then cut up into chunks and fried in olive oil, garlic, onions, potatoes, red capsicums and any other vegetables or also as a frittata.

This was then eaten with crusty pane di casa.

This was our breakfast!

It was *"molto deliciouso"*, very delicious!

Three vintage buses

Chapter 9: Sydney: *A Simpler Time!*

"Those Were the Days"

Once upon a time there was a tavern
Where we used to raise a glass or two
Remember how we laughed away the hours
And think of all the great things we would do
Those were the days my friend
We thought they'd never end
We'd sing and dance forever and a day
We'd live the life we choose
We'd fight and never lose
For we were young and sure to have our way
La la la la la la
La la la la la la
La la la la La la la la la la
Then the busy years went rushing by us
We lost our starry notions on the way
If by chance I'd see you in the tavern
We'd smile at one another and we'd say
Those were the days my friend
We thought they'd never end
We'd sing and dance forever and a day
We'd live the life we choose
We'd fight and never lose
Those were the days, oh yes those were the days
La la la la la la
La la la la la la
La la la la La la la la la la

Just tonight I stood before the tavern
Nothing seemed the way it used to be
In the glass I saw a strange reflection
Was that lonely woman really me
Those were the days my friend
We thought they'd never end
We'd sing and dance forever and a day
We'd live the life we choose
We'd fight and never lose
Those were the days, oh yes those were the days
La la la la la la
La la la la la la
La la la la La la la la la la
la la la la la la
La la la la la la
La la la la La la la la la la
Through the door there came familiar laughter
I saw your face and heard you call my name
Oh my friend we're older but no wiser
For in our hearts the dreams are still the same
Those were the days my friend
We thought they'd never end
We'd sing and dance forever and a day
We'd live the life we choose
We'd fight and never lose
Those were the days, oh yes those were the days
La la la la la la
La la la la la la
La la la la La la la la la la
La la la la la la
La la la la la la
La la la la La la la la la la

Sung by: *Mary Hopkin*
Songwriter: Gene Raskin

Sydney was a much more innocent and simpler place in the 1960s. On Saturdays *ALL* shops closed at midday and night shopping…forget about it! Of course, *EVERYTHING* was closed on Sundays! Sunday was reserved for family!

My father tried to work as much overtime as possible to earn more money. Overtime was paid at penalty rates, which was time and a half, double time or even triple time. This was very desirable. He worked overtime most evenings (paid at time and a half) and half a day some Saturdays (paid at double time). Sundays (paid at triple time) was very rare.

When he worked on a Saturday and he was in good mood, he would bring back half a cooked pigs head (boiled by the butcher). The pigs head was completely cut vertically in half. Half a brain, one eye, one ear, half a tongue etc. He bought this at *"Caminiti's Butcher"* the corner of Great North Road and Henry Street Five Dock, opposite where the old post office used to be. *"Caminiti's"* is still there, now run by the son. The post office is no longer there and the building lies empty and abandoned!

Butchers in those days all had saw dust on the floor to collect any blood that was dropped. All the meat was wrapped up in butcher's paper and everything was fresh.

The pigs' heads were piled in a heap in the window of the butcher's shop and they were very cheap. When my father arrived home with the pig's head wrapped up in butcher's paper we knew that he had had a good day and that we were going to have good afternoon.

He spread it out on the red Formica kitchen table and red plastic covered chairs, like a proud hunter returning from his kill. We all sat around the boiled head devouring it like Vikings.

We were one family in this moment!

Everyone was happy!

The pigs head was *"molto deliciouso"*!

After having our fill and being satiated with our meal, we all went off for an afternoon siesta.

The house was quiet!

The house at this moment was a *"home"*!

We also had fresh bread *(Vienna, pane di casa)* delivered to us every weekday and seven loaves on a Friday to last the whole weekend. We loved our bread. We ate bread with everything, even with pasta, especially with pasta, when we would dunk the crusty bread into the *"ragu"*, wiping every last bit from the plate. We were big eaters!

Once a week *"Giovanni a'Spezza"* would come around his small trunk laden with all manner of delicacies, eggs, pasta, cheese, salami, fruit, he had it all. He owned a grocery store in Haberfield, the neighbouring suburb, but once a week he would drive around, selling his produce to Italians. He was a short, old, balding, grey haired man. What made him unusual though, was that he only had one arm! His left arm had been cut off at the shoulder. He was able to manage very well with just his right arm, which I found very impressive. I never asked him directly what had happened to his left arm, but the story that was told was that he had tried to escape from a prison camp in the war and that the Germans cut off his arm as an example to the other prisoners. I think it worked!

We also had fresh milk home delivered every morning by the *"milkman"*.

We bought our first black and white television set in 1968. It was a very exciting time. The TV was a modular, top of the range Kriesler 36" CRT and was the centrepiece of the lounge room. It changed my life FOREVER! Nothing was ever the same after getting the TV!

My favourite TV shows were:

- Bonanza
- The Mod Squad
- Mission Impossible
- The Big Valley
- Batman
- Bewitched
- I Dream of Jeannie
- Green Acres
- Petticoat Junction
- My Three Sons
- The Many Loves of Dobie Gillis
- Gilligan's Island
- I Spy
- The Man from UNCLE
- The Saint
- Cheyenne

"The Ballad of Daniel Boone"

Daniel Boone was a man. Yes a big man.
With an eye like an eagle and as tall as a mountain was he.
Daniel Boone was a man. Yes a big man.

From the coonskin cap on the top of ol' Dan to the heel of his rawhide shoe
The rippin'est roarin'est fightin'est man the frontier ever knew.

Daniel Boone was a man. Yes a big man.

What a Boone. What a dooer. What a dream come a truer was he.

Songwriters: Vera Matson and Lionel Newman

- Daniel Boone
- Jim Bowie
- The Phantom Agents (10:00am on a Saturday morning)
- Dangerman
- Prisoner
- Thunderbirds
- Captain Scarlet
- The Waltons

- The Beverly Hillbillies
- Star Trek
- Maverick
- Brian Henderson's Bandstand (at 6:30pm on a Saturday night straight after the 6 O'clock news)
- The Bobby Limb Variety Show (at 7:320pm on a Friday night)
- Reg Lindsay's Country and Western Hour (at 1:00pm on a Saturday arvo)
- Nock and Kirby's Joe the Gadget Man
- Wrestling (at 12:00 midday on a Saturday)
- Sunday afternoon Football (they only televised the 2nd half and the commentators were Ron Casey and Rex *"Moose"* Mossop)

My favourite cartoons were:

- The Flintstones
- Marine Boy
- Prince Planet
- Rocky and Bullwinkle
- Superman
- Spiderman
- Marvel Super Heroes
- Gigantor
- The Magilla Gorilla Show
- Fractured Fairy Tales

We bought it from *"John Whitford's Family Store"*, in Five Dock owned by *"John Whitford"*. In fact, we bought everything from "Whitford's" because it had EVERYTHING! You could buy whatever you wanted there, furniture, electrical and whitegoods. It's still there today as *"John Whitford's Electrical Discount Store"* run by his sons. This was where I used to see and closely study my father's incredible haggling skills. He was a master at it. It was at the same time beautiful and excruciatingly painful to watch and experience. Truly *"A Dance Macabre"*! He would only negotiate with John himself and John was your typical Aussie bloke, very kind, warm, inviting and honest to the core. The final stages of the dance were very beautiful. John would put out his hand and say, *"Ok Joe, you have a deal!"* and there would be handshakes and big smiles all round. *John Whitford* was a great bloke!

"Whitford's" was located on *"Great North Road"*, the main road through Five Dock. I never understood what was so *"Great"* about it and it wasn't even that

long, running only about three kilometres from Parramatta Road at its south to Abbottsford Point at its north. Along it, was Five Dock shopping centre in which I would spend a lot of my time. One of my favourite stores was *"Coles Variety Store"*, located at the very southern end of the shopping centre. It no longer exists! The layout was very simple, one large counter in the centre of the store which contained an aisle for the sales staff to be in, broken half way down the store, creating two walking aisles and four rows of merchandise.

This is where I bought my first LP record of *"The Beatles Greatest Hits"*. I was very excited and rushed to play it on our new record player that my brother had proudly bought for the household. When I put it on you can imagine my disappointment when, it was NOT The Beatles but *"Bert Kaempfert plays The Beatles Greatest Hits on piano"*!

One of the most inspirational, amazing and transformative events for me, that would set my imagination racing for the rest of my life, occurred on a cold and wet July morning. I was in 4th class of primary school and the whole school was ushered into the school hall to sit down on the cold wooden floor and watch a very small black and white television screen. I remember it clearly. I was seated quite close, about four rows from the front, so I had an excellent view of the screen. We sat there from 9:00 am and even had recess and lunch there. We were not allowed to go anywhere. This was a very big occasion. It was a world changing occasion. The date was July 21st, 1969. *"The Moon Landing!"*

Then it happened, about 1:00pm. I watched in utter astonishment and amazement, Neil Armstrong climb gingerly down the ladder of "The Eagle" to be the first human being EVER to set foot on another world in or solar system. When he took his first steps on the surface of The Moon, in the *"Sea of Tranquility"* and spoke those now awe inspiring words:

"One small step for man, one giant leap for mankind!".

Those words, spoken by Neil Armstrong, still now, bring a chill and a tingle down my spine!

I felt one with humanity!

I knew then, humans could achieve ANYTHING! That even with all the hatred and wars in the world, I felt that if we could achieve this amazing feat, we could, one day overcome these as well.

I was filled with joy and happiness.

I was ten years old!

I watched as the camera panned the desolate lunar landscape. Enthralled by the achievement and pondered at what they must have been feeling and thinking as they watched planet Earth from afar, possibly to never return home. Like other previous adventurers and explorers that discovered new worlds on Earth, they had ventured where no human had EVER been before and in so doing risked their own lives for the advancement of human dreams, curiosity and knowledge.

> "Space, the final frontier
> These are the voyages of the Starship Enterprise.
> Its five years mission,
> To explore strange new worlds,
> To seek out new life,
> And new civilizations,
> To boldly go where no man has gone before!"
>
> "Star Trek Classic"

This started my lifelong interest in:

- *science fiction,*
- *space,*
- *space exploration*
- *space colonization,*
- *technology,*
- *extra-terrestrials,*
- *aliens,*
- *alien lifeforms,*
- *cosmology,*
- *philosophy,*
- *The meaning in/of life,*
- *Eastern philosophy and religions,*
- *Synchronicity,*
- *Singularity,*
- *augmentation,*
- *cybernetics,*
- *HuBots,*
- *Artificial Intelligence (AI) and*
- *artificial lifeforms!*

"Armstrong"

Black boy in Chicago
Playing in the street
Not enough to wear
Not near enough to eat
But don't you know he saw-aw it
On a July afternoon
Saw a man named Armstrong
Walk upon the moon

Young girl in Calcutta
Barely eight years old
The flies that swarm the market place
Will she don't get old
Don't you know she heard it
On a July afternoon
Heard a man named Armstrong
Walk upon the moon
Heard a man named Armstrong
Walk upon the moon

The rivers getting dirty
The wind is getting bad
War and hate are killing off
The only Earth we have
But the world all stopped to watch it
On that July afternoon
To watch a man named Armstrong
Walk upon the moon
To watch a man named Armstrong
Walk upon the moon

And I wonder if a long time ago
Somewhere in the universe
They watched a man named Adam
Walk upon the Earth.

Performed by: Reg Lindsay
Songwriter: John Stewart

The Earth as seen from The Moon.
Photo: Thanks to Facebook, friend
Malena Palomino

I became enthralled by space, science fiction. I began to read science fiction, my favourite author was and still is today, John Wyndham. To me, he was the "father" of science fiction. Most of the greatest and most iconic themes, that have been used over and over again, in science fiction, came from his imagination! *"The Day of the Triffids"*, *"The Midwich Cuckoos"*, *"The Trouble with Lichen"*, *"The Kraken Wakes"*, *"The Chrysalids"*, *"Chocky"*.

Christmas holidays were especially a bad time for me because they would invariably coincide with my father's four weeks annual leave. This meant doing work around the house such as painting, fixing the roof, fixing the fence, there always seemed something that my father would find to fix. I would be required to be on standby and be on call at a moments notice. This could include hold the ladder whist he cleaned the gutters. This was particularly distressing because he would only wear shorts and if I ever looked up I got an eyeful of his testicles in all their wrinkled glory.

A VERY disturbing sight I assure you!

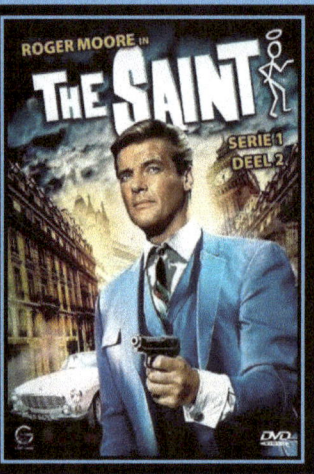

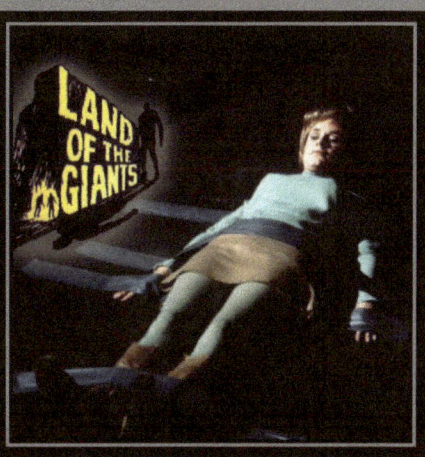
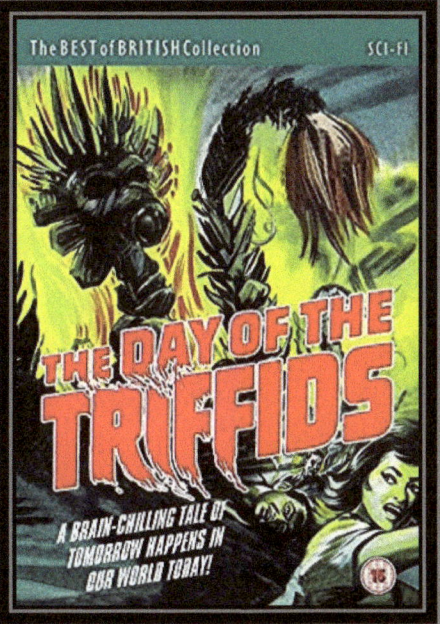

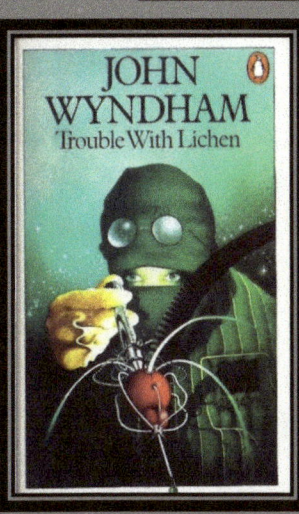

Previous page: TV shows (L to R):
The Prisoner, The Saint, The Waltons, The Many Loves of Dobie Gilies,
Star Trek, The Outer Limits, The Twilight Zone, UFO, Voyage to the Bottom of the Sea.
This Page: More TV shows (L to R):
Bonanza, Daniel Boone, Land of the Giants
Science Fiction Titles by John Wyndham (L to R):
The Day of the Triffids, The Midwich Cuckoos, The Chrysalids,
The Kraken Wakes, Trouble with Lichen

What one has to understand is that my father was not a handyman. He could not fix things. What could be done in ten minutes would take him four hours and the end result was SHIT!

The other distressing thing was waiting for him to call out *"pilyama a'caussa!"*, "get me the thing!". Panic would immediately set in. What thing? I would feverishly look around me looking to see if anything was obvious. There was not! I knew he was getting irritated.

> ### "When I Was Young"
>
> The rooms were so much colder then
> My father was a soldier then
> And times were very hard
> When I was young
> I smoked my first cigarette at ten
> And for girls, I had a bad yen
> And I had quite a ball
> When I was young
> When I was young, it was more important
> Pain more painful
> Laughter much louder
> Yeah, when I was young
> When I was young
> I met my first love at thirteen
> She was brown and I was pretty green
> And I learned quite a lot when I was young
> When I was young
> When I was young
> It was more important
> Pain more painful
> Laughter much louder
> Yeah, when I was young
> When I was young
> My faith was so much stronger then
> I believed in fellow men
> And I was so much older then
> When I was young
> When I was young
> When I was young
>
> Performed by: <u>The Animals</u>
> Songwriter: Eric Victor Burdon

Chapter 10: Death, God, Religion, Love and Masturbation!

"Red Right Hand"

Take a little walk to the edge of town
And go across the tracks
Where the viaduct looms
Like a bird of doom
As it shifts and cracks
Where secrets lie in the border fires
In the humming wires
Hey man, you know
You're never coming back

Past the square, past the bridge
Past the mills, past the stacks
On a gathering storm comes
A tall handsome man
In a dusty black coat with
A red right hand

He'll wrap you in his arms,
Tell you that you've been a good boy
He'll rekindle all the dreams
It took you a lifetime to destroy
He'll reach deep into the hole
Heal your shrinking soul
But there won't be a single thing that you can do

He's a god, he's a man
He's a ghost, he's a guru
They're whispering his name
Through this disappearing land
But hidden in his coat
Is a red right hand

You don't have no money?
He'll get you some
You don't have no car?
He'll get you one
You don't have no self-respect
You feel like an insect
Well don't you worry buddy
'Cause here he comes
Through the ghettos and the barrio
And the Bowery and the slum
A shadow is cast wherever he stands
Stacks of green paper in his
Red right hand

You'll see him in your nightmares
You'll see him in your dreams
He'll appear out of nowhere but
He ain't what he seems
You'll see him in your head
On the TV screen
Hey buddy, I'm warning
You to turn it off
He's a ghost, he's a god
He's a man, he's a guru
You're one microscopic cog
In his catastrophic plan
Designed and directed by
His red right hand

Performed by: Nick Cave and The Bad Seeds
Songwriters: Mick Harvey / Nick Cave / Thomas Wydler

My first girl I had a crush on was Gayle Saunders. She was the most beautiful girl to me. I drooled over her. We were both in the same class. She, on the other hand, favoured a new boy called Shane' who had just come to our school. I was so jealous of Shane. He was and had all the things that I didn't and wanted. He was an Aussie *(a "Skip")*, had straight, long blond hair and was very popular with the girls. They ALL drooled over him. I on the other hand was a *"Wog"*, had curly, short red hair with huge freckles all over my face. I always wished to be an Aussie, for long, straight black or blonde hair and be popular with girls. I was delusional!

One day I decided to let her know how I felt, so I decided to write her a note. A simple, brief and straight to the point note; *"I love YOU!"*. I gave it to Deborah Hatcher to deliver to Gayle. BIG mistake! Of course she opened it, read it and passed it around to everyone else. Gayle was the last to receive it and when she did, she came straight over to me and was very angry, saying how could I do this to her. It was another one of those moments that I wished I could have had the superpower of *"Teleportation"*, so that I could instantaneously disappear!

I was NEVER lucky with *"LOVE"*!

Death was always a huge preoccupation for me. I never really knew why but I was always interested in what happened to you when you died. I'd lay awake in bed, in the darkness, sometimes with the sheets over my head and imagine myself dying. Was it like complete darkness? Was it like going to sleep and NEVER waking up? The only place to find answers to these questions was GOD!

I went to church, *"All Hallows Catholic Church"* in Five Dock every Sunday morning. Afterwards I went across the road to the Catholic Primary School, to attend Sunday School and learn teachings from the bible run by the nuns. I went for a couple of reasons not all spiritual and altruistic. It got me out of the house for at least 3 hours every Sunday from 7:00am to 10:00am. Nevertheless, I did become very religious and started to believe in a higher power, one who was omnipotent, listened to your problems and could fix them if you prayed and believed hard enough. I became very religious. I prayed all the time! I had many problems that needed fixing!

On one cold, bleak, windy and rainy school morning we were playing; *who could climb the netball posts the fastest*, in the enclosed bubbler and wash area. As always, I was very competitive and sprang onto the pole like a polecat eager to get to the top and touch the ring. I was wearing shorts, I was about half way up when I started to experience very strange and unusual sensations in my penis as I was rubbing against the pole. I was very disturbed and shocked. In fact, I became quite disoriented. I reached the top and stayed there for a short time trying to figure what had just happened and get my breath back. I started to slide down and there was the sensation again. I decided that I had injured my dick somehow, but I could not tell anyone. I had to keep quiet! I prayed to God that I was alright!

That night in bed I decided to rub my dick and continue rubbing it. The sensation was like something I had never experienced before. It was FANTASTIC! The more I kept rubbing, the more I couldn't stop. Until, finally to my utter astonishment I felt like an explosion was taking over my whole body. I started shuddering, convulsing and then without warning a white fluid squirted out of my dick all over me! What the fuck had I done! Had I ruptured something? Oh God, I should've stopped when I had the chance! I was being punished! I had been bad! I turned to God! I prayed for God to save me because I was a sinner and I had sinned BIG time, to the point of rupturing some vital organ in my body! I was gonna DIE!

I told GOD that I would NEVER do that AGAIN!

But I was weak!

I succumbed to the DEVIL!

To TEMPTATION!

I was WEAK!

Every night I would succumb!

Every night I would REPENT!

I was ASHAMED at how weak I was!

One afternoon, Nick abruptly opened my bedroom door without knocking and caught me in the act. I started to cry at being caught. He just laughed and said *"Don't worry Vic, everyone does it! It's natural!"*.

With those few words, the world was back to normal again!

Chapter 11: Family Time! A Bonding Time! Just an Ordinary Aussie Family

"We Are Family"

We are family
I got all my sisters with me
We are family
Get up everybody and sing

We are family
I got all my sisters with me
We are family
Get up everybody and sing

I got my sisters with me
Everybody, hey hey hey
Get up, get up and sing it to me
We're having fun
Life, life has just begun for me
Me, me and my family
Get up, get up and sing it
Sing it, sing it, sing it, sing it to me
Yeah, we're back together like birds of a feather
Get up, come on y'all

We are family (Hey, y'all)
I got all my sisters with me
We are family
Get up everybody and sing (sing it to me)

We are family
I got all my sisters with me
We are family
Get up everybody and sing

Performed by: Sister Sledge
Songwriters: Nile Rodgers / Bernard Edwards

Weekends were 'Family Time". Time which was spent with my parents doing and making things.

I hated weekends!

I hated *"Family Time"!*

I would do anything to escape, even go to church!

This *"Family Time"* could be going to markets and getting chickens *(something I really loved……..NOT!)*. Other activities which I also really looked forward to and loved, happened once a year. These included:

- **Bottling Tomatoes**

    This happened in the month of January and could either take place on one day or it could be stretched out over a couple of weekends depending on the supply of overripe *"Roma"* tomatoes. They had to be *"Roma"* tomatoes because their shape was very important in this process, and a process it was indeed.

    First just a few boxes of *"Roma"* tomatoes had to be brought from the markets, only about thirty boxes give or take. Then came the extremely laborious work of cutting up the *"Roma"* tomatoes into long strips. This was so they could be easily inserted into *"beer"* bottles which had a narrow mouth and neck!

    Everybody was given a dedicated job. This was a production line. There were the cutters, who sliced up the *"Roma"* tomatoes. This was done on a large, thick wooden board. Then there were the bottle fillers, they put the slices of *"Roma"* tomatoes with leaves of *"basil"*, into the *"beer"* bottles. Lastly was the most important and difficult job of all……capping the bottles with a bottle cap.

    Capping was done mechanically using a hammer and a cushion upon which the bottle was placed. The procedure was very simple, place the filled bottle of tomatoes onto the cushion, place the bottle top onto the bottle, a piece of wood with a metal cap was place onto the bottle top, hit the piece of wood with the hammer.

    This was my job *(oh lucky me!)*

    As you may realise this was fraught with danger!

    The hitting had to be carried out with exact force. Use too much force and the bottle would shatter!

This was the worst case scenario!

This was to be avoided at all costs!

Use not enough force and you would have to repeat the procedure but this time your confidence had been dented because of the previous failure, stress levels increased!

I was traumatised!

I guess I should have been proud to have been given such an important job. It probably meant I had the lowest number of breakages. I was the BEST!

It didn't make me feel any better.

Finally, when all the *"Roma"* tomatoes had been sliced and all the 200 or so bottles capped, it was time to sterilise the *"Roma"* tomatoes. This was done by heating a huge cauldron of water, putting the bottles into it and gently heating it, making sure the water never boiled because this could also shatter the bottles. I was not involved in this part *(thank God!)*.

These bottled tomatoes were used to make the most delicious pasta sauce!

- **Making Wine**

Making wine was another joyous event for me…. BUT especially for my father. This took place late March towards the end of summer, when the last and cheapest grapes became available. The whole process was very long and laborious. There was a pre-preparation week, the actual day of production and a post-production week of duties to be carried out! My job was to *"the goffer"*. That is, to do whatever the fuck my father wanted me to. Sometimes, I swear, he just got me to do things just for his own amusement because they made absolutely no fucking logical sense to me. I was basically his little slave to be ever ready, on standby for his call!!!

The pre-preparation week involved washing out all the wooden barrels, the grape press, the many containers, the glass flagons and setting up all the equipment ready for the BIG day.

The grapes had been ordered a couple of months earlier from *"Merlino"*, an Italian guy who was the middle man, organising the purchase, transport and delivery of the grapes to our home in a small ute. He would organise a semi-trailer laden with boxes of grapes from the Barossa Valley, South Australia to come to Five Dock for maybe twenty or thirty other families from the area. My father would always order the same quantity of boxes of grapes, twenty five boxes of black grapes (usually Cabernet) and five boxes of white grapes (usually Waltham Cross), based on an average amount of wine produced per box and the size of his containers to store it in.

The actual day of wine making started early, about 5:30am, nothing unusual in that! My father was very keen to make sure that everything was prepared and ready for the delivery, and he had given strict instructions to *"Merlino il'cantiniere"* that he wanted first delivery. So, we were all put on *"battle-stations"*, ready for action at any moment! When the ute finally arrived, everyone sprang into action. We all knew what to do. We had done this many times before. It was as if it was imprinted into our DNA. The boxes had to be unloaded and taken to the backyard of the house and pilled next to our next door neighbour's (*Mr Brailley*) fence. The boxes were made of wood and so were quite heavy, containing on average anywhere between twenty or thirty kilograms of grapes. Later on the boxes were made from polystyrene which made them slightly lighter. My father would at this stage check out the quality of the grapes and decide if the wine was going to be any good or not and whether they would produce a good yield. He would look at the size and quality of the grapes, if they were large and plump, this meant a good yield but very weak wine, too much water. If they were small and plump, this meant a small yield but a good alcohol content, optimal was 13% alcohol. If they were shrivelled and dried *"appassolito"*, this meant a very low yield but a very high alcohol content (possibly as high as 16%), this meant that the wine would be very strong and be very dark in colour. My father preferred a light, easy drinking wine rather than a heavy *"Shiraz"*.

Now the actual work started, crushing the grapes!

Initially this was carried out using our feet in an old enamelled bathtub with claw feet, the ones that are now very sought after and very expensive, but actually this was a very inefficient method and was quickly replaced by a mechanical crushing machine. It consisted of a handle which turned two gears attached to two interlocking solid cylindrical gears which could be adjusted to vary the crushing strength for different sized grapes, to cater for small or large grapes which foot stomping could not. There were a lot of whole grapes left in the brew using feet. This was all but eliminated when using the crushing machine.

The machine was now placed onto the bathtub which collected the crushed grapes and brew. It could be filled with a couple of boxes and then the crushing started by turning the hand using brute, human strength. Initially, it was enough for gravity and the weight of the grapes to feed the cogs but most times, the grapes needed help to be fed into the cogs and this is where a closed fist or a large piece of wood came in handy.

My job alternated between carrying the boxes of grapes and filling the crushing machine to turning the handle of the crushing machine. Usually this turned into a competition to see who could crush a box of grapes the fastest. I of course was always the fastest. NO ONE could BEAT ME! I think I could crush a full box of grapes within thirty seconds! Pretty IMPRESSIVE!

The crushing of the grapes was actually the easy and mostly fun part of the day! We could crush all thirty boxes of grapes in about one hour!

The crushed grapes with all the juice was put into a very large wooden press (*"Il torquo"*), a mechanical separating machine. This was made from a very heavy, round metal base with a lip at some point on it is circumference and a metal pole attached in the middle which had a screw at the free end where a rotating head onto which a metal lever (basically a long metal pole) was inserted. Two wooden vertically slatted cages, with gaps between the slats, were then connected together to make a frame structure. This was filled with the crushed grapes and juice and then wooden blocks were placed on top, with the metal head wound to press down, allowing all the grape juice to flow out the lip but retain the grape skins, seeds and stalks inside. The grape juice was collected in a bucket and then transferred into a twenty five litre or larger container made from wood or later from plastic, where the fermentation process would occur.

This kept on going until ALL the crushed grapes and juice were in the press and no more juice could be pressed out of them. This was grape juice, which was a cloudy purple red colour and very sweet and sticky.

Next came the tedious parts of the process! ALL the stalks had to be removed from the crushed grapes and only the grape skins were left. Then a bucket of these grape skins was put into each of the containers of wine juice. Then a piece of fine wire mesh was placed over the mouth of the container. The reason for removing the grape stalks was that to put these into the grape juice would change the flavour of the wine and my father wanted an easy drinking wine, not too strong. He also prided himself in not adding any preservatives or stabilisers to the juice. He would proudly boast; *"Mio vino e tutti pure e natural! (My wine is totally pure and natural!)"*

The fermentation process of turning grape juice into wine had already started.

The wine containers had to be stirred regularly, at least a couple of times a day to assist and accelerate the fermentation process. You knew fermentation had started when froth started to form on top and within days the frothing would become quite vigorous and might even overflow over the top. This was why it was important not to seal the container and leave it open. The mesh allowed for this and also stopped any animals getting inside. All the added grape skins would be floating on top with the froth and the bubbles. There was also a particular smell associated with this very aggressive chemical process of turning sugars into alcohol…. wine, *"vino"*, which I can smell clearly to this very day! I know it and can recognise it ANYWHERE! The smell of FERMENTATION!

After about seven days, the frothing had stopped, the grape skins had fallen to the bottom of the container, the wine was almost clear, quite drinkable and the process was complete. But the wine was too young *"troppo giovane"*, to drink straight away. It was now decanted from the containers, the sludge and the grape skins on the bottom and placed in receptacles, either wooden barrels or glass *"damiganni"*, which my father preferred and sealed for up to three months. This was the clarifying stage. In this stage the wine became crystal clear and separated from any particulates, which settle to the bottom as sludge due to gravity. These containers were stored in a cool location usually in a cellar or *"cantina"*. This was very important because if the wine became too hot, the fermentation process would start again in the containers and the wine would become *"Acetic Acid"*…. Vinegar…. Wine Vinegar!

After three months the wine was ready to drink and be decanted and transferred into four litre flagons (about fifty of them). He was very proud of his wine and drank it every day. I only drank it if I was desperate. I was desperate a lot!

The bottles of tomatoes and flagons of wine were kept under the house because we didn't have a cellar and was the coolest place of the house. Access was very restricted as there was only about 80cm height above the ground so it was my job to crawl on all fours under the house. It was tight even for me, but I persevered. It wasn't too bad. We'd put pieces of cardboard on the ground so I didn't get soiled, as the ground was just bare earth as you'd expect under the floorboards of a house. In fact, under the house there was a level of tranquility and serenity that I didn't get above the floorboards, which I enjoyed!

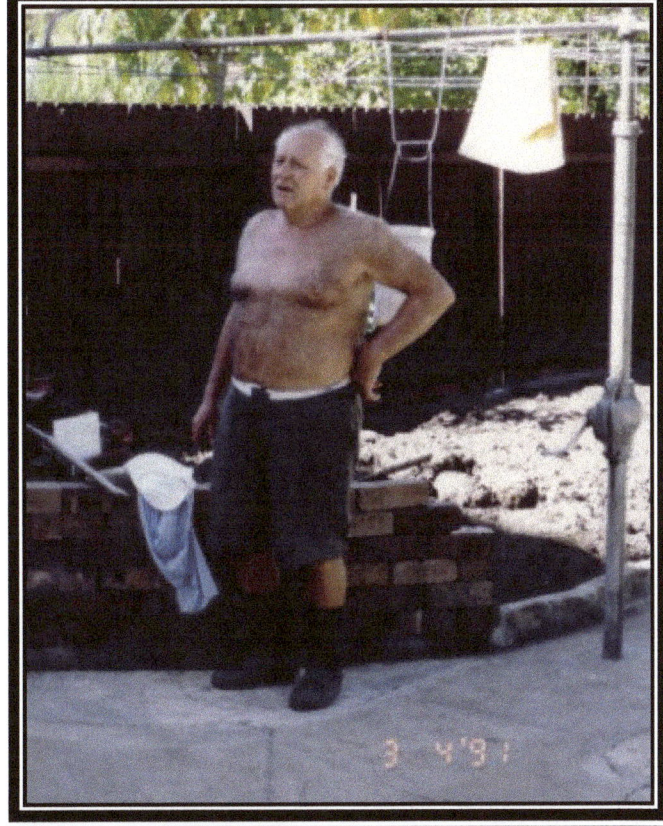

Wine Making
1: Father
2: Father

Photos circa 1990

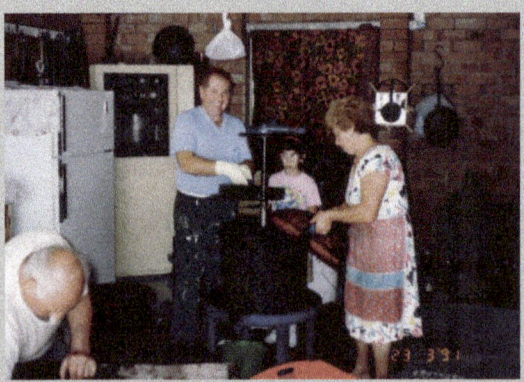

Wine Making
1: Father
2: Mother
3: Nick and mother
4: Father, Nick, mother and niece Michelle
5: Father, Nick, Michelle and mother
6: Father, Nick and Michelle
7: Father, Nick, Michele and mother

Photos circa 1990

I don't know how it came about but in one particular year, my dad came out by stating that, women who were menstruating could not participate in the wine making process. Apparently, their involvement would turn the wine into vinegar! What a load of horse-shit I thought to myself. Another one of his crazy-arsed superstitious beliefs or myths that some old fart had told him. I thought to myself, this is bullshit, my mother has been making wine with us and she's a woman, I think?

Then one day I remembered that when I was very young, she had a hysterectomy!

1 & 2: Wine containers, photos July 2019
3: My mother coming back from her hysterectomy operation,   4: Nick and mother
Photos circa 1970

- **Making Salami**

Another important event in the yearly, *"Radice Famiglia"* culinary calendar was salami making. We're not talking one or two kilograms here! We're talking twenty or thirty kilograms. This was a big event, one which I didn't mind too much as, although it was a time consuming process, it wasn't too laborious. This was done in the coldest months of the year, mid July. Cold weather is an essential ingredient in the drying process. If it was too warm, the salami would not dry properly and could go off. The cold inhibited bacteria from growing inside the salami.

The meat had to be pork. Pork was important because of its fat content. The meat could not be lean. One of the most important factors to making good and tasty salami was the fat content. The meat had to be fatty otherwise it would be too tough and unable to be eaten. It would be like *"prosciutto"* or *"copa"* rather than salami. That's why butchers' have very soft hands, it's because of the fat (lard) which is in the meat and this moisturises their hands!

In the early years, we did everything ourselves, we minced the meat using a hand mincer, extra fat was added if needed, according to personal preference. Once the meat had been minced, it was placed in a big container. Now came the creative process, adding extra ingredients to personalise the salami. At this stage chilli, pepper, salt, paprika, fennel *"finocchio"* seeds all could be added to create your own particular salami, *"picante"* (hot) or "dolce" *(sweet)*. No chemical additives or preservatives was added, everything was natural! A sample was fried and tasted to see if all the ingredients worked well. I like this part, especially with a slice of crusty *"pane di casse"*, *"molto delicioso"*. Sublime!

The next step was to fill the salami skins, which are actually pig intestines! This was originally done by hand, wrapping the skin around the end of an aluminium funnel and feeding the salami mince into it, which filled the salami skin, until there was one long salami at the end of the funnel. It was very important that there were no air pockets. The salami mince had to be packed in tight, for uniformity of drying. Then, every ten centimetres or so, it was twisted was to make five or six knobs of salami. These were hung up and using a needle, the skins were randomly punctured. This was to allow the fat to escape in the smoking and drying process.

Once all the salami had been made they were hung in a smoke house. In our case it was the outside BBQ built by my father, the one with wonky sides which was converted by placing a sheet of corrugated iron as a roof and the salami was hung underneath. Every night a fire was lit but it was very important NOT to have flames, only smoke was wanted. This was very important as you did not want to cook the salami, only to dry it using smoke. The smoke also gave flavour to the salami. The fat from the salami would start to ooze out as it started to dry and it would drop on the charcoals which would produce more smoke and so the process went. This was carried out nightly for a week until the salami had shrunk and shrivelled in size quite noticeably. Now it was time to taste the salami. A nob was cut and sliced open, it should be a deep maroon colour, the slices were divvied out and placed once again on a piece of crusty *"panne di case"* and bitten into. No need for butter, the salami had taken care of all that. Heaven!

However, it didn't always work out, sometimes the weather changed and it was unseasonably warm, this is when my father would start to swear *"a va fan culo"*, *"putana"*, *"merda"*, *"porco miseria"*, were the most common ones. The most common issues were when the inside of the salami might have holes in it or it, might be a grey colour meaning it had gone off. In these cases, the only thing to do was to salvage as much of the salami as possible and throw the rest away. My father did this with gritted teeth and a knife in his heart.

He took these things very personally!

In fact, he took EVERYTHING, very personally!

Not everything was good homemade bottles of tomatoes, wine or salami and crusty *"pane di case"*, in the *"Radice Famiglia"* household!

1, 2: The backyard garden in the Five Dock house.

Photos taken by Mariclaire Pringle, 14.07.2019

Making Salami
1: Zia Donnatamaria, mother, nonna Radice, cousin Geraldine
2: Mother and Zia Rosa making "fusilli" pasta
Photos taken in Difesa, Italy 1979. Salami
3, 4, 5: Salami and wine casks in the garage in Five Dock
Photos taken by Mariclaire Pringle, June, 2019

Chapter 12: The Golden Chariot

"Roadhouse Blues"

A-keep your eyes on the road, your hand upon the wheel
Keep your eyes on the road, your hand upon the wheel
Yeah, we're goin' to the roadhouse
We're gonna have a real
A-good time

Yeah, the back of the roadhouse they got some bungalows
Yeah, the back of the roadhouse they got some bungalows
And that's for the people
Who like to go down slow

Let it roll, baby, roll
Let it roll, baby, roll
Let it roll, baby, roll
Let it roll, all night long

Do it, Robby, do it

All right
Hey, yeah

You gotta roll, roll, roll
You gotta thrill my soul, all right
Roll, roll, roll, roll
A-thrill my soul
Ya gotta beep a gonk a chucha
Honk konk konk
Da ga da beep a con ja choo chon

Honk honk honk
A don ta ee cha koo na nee cha
Bop a loo la ree chow
Bomp a kee cho ee sonk konk
Yeah, ride

Ashen lady, ashen lady
Give up your vows, give up your vows
Save our city, save our city
Right now

The Doors

And I woke up this morning, I got a-myself a beer
And I woke up this morning, and I got a-myself a beer
The future's uncertain and the end is always near

Let it roll, baby, roll
Let it roll, baby, roll
Let it roll, baby, roll
Let it roll, hey
All night long

Performed by: The Doors
Songwriter: Jim Morrison

The greatest love of my father's life was his beloved and cherished *"Golden Chariot"*, his white *"Chrysler Valiant"*. He bought it in December 1969. It had a *"Hemi 245Hp V6 engine"* complete with a red chilli and the Devils horns fingers hanging from the rear view mirror to the white rug on the rear window with the bobbing tiger's head, registration number, ADQ 498! It was built like a tank. All steel. You could drive head on into a brick wall and the brick wall would come out of it second best. That's how strong it was! It was a beast! Fast, boy was it fast.! It would leave all other cars for dead! It was a petrol guzzler though, as were all cars of that era. No saving the environment of the planet in those days.

He still did not know how to drive when he bought it and he learnt on it. The only thing he had driven before was horse or his donkey. In fact, when he was driving, he drove like he was still riding his donkey. He would heave backwards and forwards in his seat, as if to urge the car to go faster.

Being a passenger when he drove was not a pleasant or enjoyable experience. I never felt very comfortable because he was quite an erratic and impulsive driver at the best of times. He would love to give a bit of a work out every now and then when we would go out for a drive on a Sunday and take the freeway (yes, roads were actually *FREE* in those days), probably to go to farm to buy live chickens! He would love to accelerate to eighty or ninety miles per hour, it still had the Imperial Units on its speedometer, so he never was quite sure how many kilometres per hour he was actually go! He was the happiest on these occasions saying proudly, *"Abbiamo gettare?"*, *"are we going to throw it?"*. I would sit in the back which didn't have seat belts fitted and it wasn't compulsory to wear them, so I would lay flat on my back and watch the sky and the clouds wiz past as my father let the beast from its chains. He was flying! Sometimes he would fly and sing. This was when he was really happy!

My mother would tell him that he loved that car more than her. Which was absolutely true! He loved that car. Treated it like a queen. He kept it in pristine condition and whenever something was wrong with it, he never once balked at spending the money to fix it. He only used genuine *"Chrysler"* parts on it. Only the best would do for his *"Golden Chariot"* and he spent a lot of money on it over the thirty-three years that he had it.

I was with him on that terrible day when he was no longer able to renew his driver's license and could therefore no longer legally drive his beloved "Golden Chariot". It was late January 2005, he was eighty-one years old and in NSW it is a requirement to have an eyesight test every year when a person becomes eighty. His eyesight had been deteriorating rapidly but as is common, he bluffed and fudged his way through. We went together to the Five Dock Motor Registry, he drove. I could see that he was nervous. I reassured him that everything would be fine. I was hoping for a miracle. We took a ticket and waited for his name to be called. We walked up to the counter and he was asked to read out the letters on the screen projected on the back wall. Straight away he said *"D A F G K"*. I was impressed. The person behind the counter asked him, *"Mr Radice, can you see the letters on the back wall?"*, *"Yes!"*, he replied. *"Can you please read them out for me?"* *"D A F G K"*, he replied. She turned to me a said *"Does your father understand?"* *"Yes"*, I replied. It's then I realised what he was doing, he had memorised letters from somewhere else and thought he could get away with it. He started to panic and tremble. *"Aiutami"*, "help me" he said to me. *"Non posso, papa!"*, *"I can't dad!"*. He started to cry. I drove his beloved *"Golden Chariot"* back home to Elizabeth Street. Old age is a *"Shithole"*!

He did drive it again a few times, illegally, mainly to *"All Hallows Church"* for Saturday evening mass. He sold it a neighbour a couple of months later and he cried again.

My father (seated inside "The White Chariot"), me and mother in front of the Five Dock house

1: Father, mother and Nick   2: Nick (inside), Zio Michaele, father   3: Me, mother and father
4: Father   5: Nick, me, Zia Laura, mother and father
All photos circa 1970

Chapter 13: In the End……

"The End"

This is the end
Beautiful friend
This is the end
My only friend, the end

Of our elaborate plans, the end
Of everything that stands, the end
No safety or surprise, the end
I'll never look into your eyes...again

Can you picture what will be
So limitless and free
Desperately in need...of some...stranger's hand
In a...desperate land

Lost in a Roman...wilderness of pain
And all the children are insane
All the children are insane
Waiting for the summer rain, yeah

There's danger on the edge of town
Ride the King's highway, baby
Weird scenes inside the gold mine
Ride the highway west, baby

Ride the snake, ride the snake
To the lake, the ancient lake, baby
The snake is long, seven miles
Ride the snake...he's old, and his skin is cold

The west is the best
The west is the best
Get here, and we'll do the rest

The bus is callin' us
The blue bus is callin' us
Driver, where you taken' us

The killer awoke before dawn, he put his boots on
He took a face from the ancient gallery
And he walked on down the hall
He went into the room where his sister lived, and...then he
Paid a visit to his brother, and then he
He walked on down the hall, and
And he came to a door...and he looked inside
Father, yes son, I want to kill you
Mother...I want to...fuck you

C'mon baby, take a chance with us
C'mon baby, take a chance with us
C'mon baby, take a chance with us
And meet me at the back of the blue bus
Doin' a blue rock
On a blue bus
Doin' a blue rock
C'mon, yeah

Kill, kill, kill, kill, kill, kill

This is the end
Beautiful friend
This is the end
My only friend, the end

It hurts to set you free
But you'll never follow me
The end of laughter and soft lie

This is the end

Performed by: The Doors
Lyrics by: Jim Morrison

My father died in the early hours of the 25th May 2008 at RPA Hospital in Camperdown, after a short illness. He was eighty-three years old. He had contracted *"septicaemia (sepsis)"* and it had spread throughout his body resulting in massive organ failure. There My father died in the early hours of 25th May 2008 at RPA hospital in Camperdown, after a short illness. He had contracted *"septicaemia (sepsis)"* and it had spread throughout his whole body resulting in massive organ failure. There was nothing the doctors could do except pump him with antibiotics which prolonged his life for an extra three weeks. Watching him die in those last weeks, I learnt that it's better to come to terms with your demons put them to rest earlier in your life, when you can. Have the strength and courage to confront them, rather than wait and fight with them when you're dying. My father was fighting his demons right till the end.

It was NOT a good death!

My mother is eighty-seven years young and is still living, by herself, in the family home in Elizabeth Street, Five Dock.

Make sure to have a good LIFE, so that you can have a good DEATH!

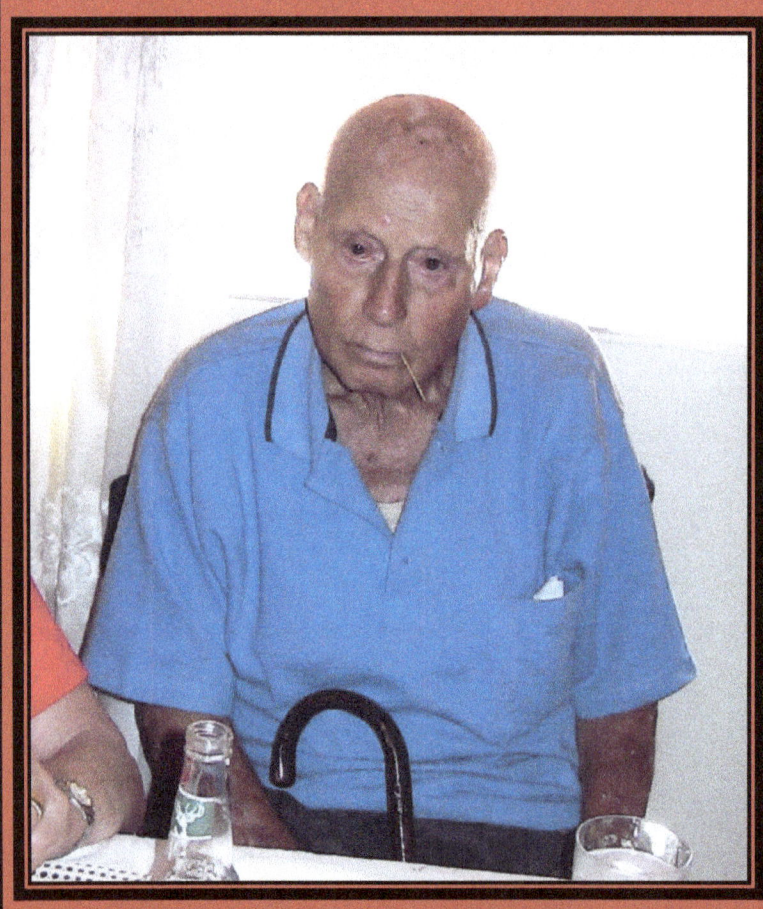

My father, Giuseppe Radice (1924-2008)
Circa Nov' 2007

My mother, Angela (Martone) Radice (1932-)
Photo taken by Lina, 05.05.2019

The End

"First of May"

When I was small, and Christmas trees were tall
We used to love while others used to play
Don't ask me why, but time has passed us by
Someone else moved in from far away

Now we are tall, and Christmas trees are small
And you don't ask the time of day
But you and I, our love will never die
But guess we'll cry come first of May

The apple tree that grew for you and me
I watched the apples falling one by one
And I recall the moment of them all
The day I kissed your cheek and you were mine

Now we are tall, and Christmas trees are small
And you don't ask the time of day
But you and I, our love will never die
But guess we'll cry come first of May

When I was small, and Christmas trees were tall
Do do do do do do do do do
Don't ask me why, but time has passed us by
Someone else moved in from far away

Performed by: The Bee Gees

Songwriters: Barry Gibb / Maurice Ernest Gibb / Robin Hugh Gibb

"Desiderata"

"Go placidly amid the noise and haste,
and remember what peace there may be in silence.
As far as possible, without surrender,
be on good terms with all persons.

Speak your truth quietly and clearly;
and listen to others,
even to the dull and ignorant;
they too have their story.

Avoid loud and aggressive persons;
they are vexations to the spirit.

If you compare yourself with others,
you may become vain or bitter,
for always there will be greater
and lesser persons than yourself.

Enjoy your achievements as well as your plans.
Keep interested in your own career, however humble,
it's a real possession in the changing fortunes of time.

Exercise caution in your business affairs,
for the world is full of trickery.
But let this not blind you to what virtue there is;
many persons strive for high ideals,
and everywhere life is full of heroism.

Be yourself.
Especially do not feign affection.
Neither be cynical about love;
for in the face of all aridity and disenchantment,
it is as perennial as the grass."

"Take kindly the counsel of the years,
gracefully surrendering the things of youth.

Nurture strength of spirit
to shield you in sudden misfortune.
But do not distress yourself with dark imaginings.
Many fears are born of fatigue and loneliness.

Beyond a wholesome discipline,
be gentle with yourself.
You are a child of the universe
no less than the trees and the stars;
you have a right to be here.
And whether or not it is clear to you,
no doubt the universe is unfolding as it should.

Therefore be at peace with God,
whatever you conceive him to be.
And whatever your labours and aspirations,
in the noisy confusion of life,
keep peace in your soul.

With all its sham, drudgery and broken dreams,
it is still a beautiful world.
Be cheerful.
Strive to be happy."

Performed by: Les Crane
Author - Max Ehrmann (1872 - 1945)

www.ingramcontent.com/pod-product-compliance
Lightning Source LLC
Chambersburg PA
CBHW041714290426
44110CB00024B/2829